Catalog
of the
Musical Works
of
William Billings

CATALOG
OF THE
MUSICAL WORKS
OF
WILLIAM BILLINGS

Compiled by
KARL KROEGER

Music Reference Collection, Number 32

GP

GREENWOOD PRESS
New York • Westport, Connecticut • London

Library of Congress Cataloging-in-Publication Data

Kroeger, Karl.
  Catalog of the musical works of William Billings / compiled by
Karl Kroeger.
      p. cm.—(Music reference collection, ISSN 0736-7740 ; no.
32)
  Includes bibliographical references and indexes.
  ISBN 0-313-27827-X (alk. paper)
  1. Billings, William, 1746-1800—Bibliography.   I. Title.
II. Series.
  ML134.B582K7 1991
  016.78225'092—dc20   91-24002

British Library Cataloguing in Publication Data is available.

Library of Congress Catalog Card Number: 91-24002
ISBN: 0-313-27827-X
ISSN: 0736-7740

First published in 1991

Greenwood Press, 88 Post Road West, Westport, CT 06881
An imprint of Greenwood Publishing Group, Inc.

Printed in the United States of America

∞™

The paper used in this book complies with the
Permanent Paper Standard issued by the National
Information Standards Organization (Z39.48—1984).

10 9 8 7 6 5 4 3 2 1

Contents

Acknowledgements

Information for this catalog has been gathered over some 15 years from many sources. It would be nearly impossible to mention all of the institutions, organizations, and individuals that have assisted in the task, yet some who have played a particularly significant role should be thanked.

To Richard Crawford and Cynthia Hoover, my co-workers on the William Billings Complete Works edition, I am grateful for all of their efforts that helped bring the edition to completion and provided information for this catalog.

Thanks to Raoul and Amy Camus, Robert and Kate Keller, and Margery Lowens and her late husband Irving for both encouragement and hospitality; to Nym Cooke, Carol Oja, and Arthur Schrader for discographic assistance; to Nicholas Temperley for information from the Hymn Tune Index at the University of Illinois; and to Gillian Anderson of the Library of Congress and William Kearns of the University of Colorado for advice and criticism.

I am grateful to the staffs of the Moravian Music Foundation, The William L. Clements Library of the University of Michigan, the American Antiquarian Society, and many New-England libraries, historical societies, and archives for their assistance in many areas, and to the University of Colorado, Boulder, for its support of my research.

Introduction

William Billings was the best-known and most talented of
a group of largely self-taught composers and singing masters
active in New England during the final third of the eighteenth
century. He was born in Boston, Massachusetts, in 1746 and
died there in 1800. The son of a shopkeeper, after his
father's death in 1760, Billings was apprenticed to a tanner.
He learned the trade and practiced it at intervals throughout
his life, but Billings's great love was sacred music --
psalmody, as it was called at the time. Although he had only
a rudimentary musical education, he taught singing schools in
the general vicinity of Boston during much of his adult life
with great success and approbation. His unique abilities as
a teacher and composer were widely recognized during his
lifetime. The diarist William Bentley called him "the father
of our New England music," and after Billings's death, Bentley
eulogized him as one who "spake and sung and thought as a man
above the common abilities."[1]

Billings published six collections of his music between
1770 and 1794, as well as about a half dozen pamphlet-sized
publications containing from one to three pieces each. His

---

1. William Bentley. _The Diary of William Bentley, D.D.,
   Pastor of East Church Salem, Massachusetts._ 4 vols.
   (Salem: Essex Institute, 1905-14), II, 350-51.

first tunebook, The New-England Psalm-Singer (Boston, 1770), issued when he was only 24, was the first collection devoted exclusively to American compositions and to the music of a single American composer. Although uneven in inspiration and insecure in technique, the tunebook was extremely popular and influential. It remains one of America's most important musical documents, setting the tone for and giving direction to American psalmody for several decades following its publication.

Billings's second tunebook, The Singing Master's Assistant (Boston, 1778) was popularly known as "Billings's Best." Although billed as "an abridgement of The New-England Psalm-Singer," over half its contents were new pieces; works carried over from the earlier tunebook had been thoroughly revised. Supplied with a clear and useful introduction to the rudiments of music and a collection of pieces that generally progressed from the simple to the complex, The Singing Master's Assistant was intended as Billings's basic singing-school textbook and appeared in four editions between 1778 and about 1789.

Having supplied music for the singing school, Billings next turned his attention to the congregational singer. Music in Miniature (Boston, 1779) is a collection of his new and old pieces, along with 10 standard British psalm tunes, intended for use in church during public worship. The tunebook was printed in a small upright format, designed to be bound with a metrical psalter. It contained only pieces that could be sung by the congregation; complex music, like fuging tunes, set pieces, and anthems, was omitted.

The Psalm-Singer's Amusement (Boston 1781), Billings's fourth collection (and the third he issued in the four-year period between 1778 and 1781), addressed yet another group of singers: the musical society. Musical societies at the time were informal groups of experienced singers who met for recreational singing and practice in psalmody. Billings challenged them with a collection consisting largely of fuging tunes, set pieces, and anthems that included some of his most adventurous music.

Five years later, Billings published The Suffolk Harmony (Boston, 1786) containing mostly unpublished pieces in a less flamboyant style. Some tunes may have been composed for use by the Universalist church in Boston, for 18 poems by the Universalist poets James and John Relly were set. Whether Billings had some formal connection with the church (he was a member of the Congregational church) is unknown. All of the pieces in <u>The Suffolk Harmony</u> point toward Billings's heightened concern for tuneful melody, close integration of words and music, and a more controlled harmonic style than in earlier works.

Billings's final tunebook, <u>The Continental Harmony</u> (Boston, 1794), the only one of his publications to be printed from moveable type rather than engraved plates, was published by the printing firm of Thomas and Andrews as a charitable enterprise, sponsored by several Boston singing societies. In the early 1790s, for reasons unknown but easily surmised, Billings had reached a financial crisis, and his supporters among Boston's singers were gravely concerned. After a benefit concert given in 1790 failed to raise sufficient funds to alleviate his plight, his supporters hit upon the idea of publishing a collection of his music and giving him the profits from its sale. <u>The Continental Harmony</u> is in every way Billings's highest achievement as a composer of psalmody. It is his largest book, containing his most complex and challenging music -- a fitting apex to over a quarter century of composing and teaching.

During the 1780s and early 1790s, Billings issued a few pieces in 8- and 16-paged pamphlets. These include two versions of his most enduringly popular piece, AN ANTHEM FOR EASTER (The Lord is Ris'n Indeed). The second version, published in 1795, has a 24-measure addition inserted in the middle of the original publication of 1787. The Easter Anthem went on to be included in many later tunebooks during the 19th century, as well as in octavo editions and anthologies in the 20th century. From its first publication in 1787 to the present day, the Easter Anthem has probably never been entirely out of print.

Following his death in 1800, the popularity of Billings's music declined as a reform movement in psalmody gained momentum. By 1820, few of his psalm tunes were sung in American urban centers. However, some of his music remained popular in the rural south and on the western frontier, where singers' tastes were not as self-consciously refined as in the larger cities. In New England, Billings's free-spirited music was anathema to reform-minded church musicians, and he was held up to scorn and ridicule in their writings.   This situation continued into the early years of the present century. Following World War II, however, critical opinion of Billings and his music changed. At first, he was looked upon as a kind of pioneer and folk hero, forging a rough-hewn but independent path in a musical wilderness through the force of his own personality and vision. Recent research, however, has balanced the picture. He is now considered as a talented and resourceful composer in a musical style quite different from the art and dance music of his day, a style which he mastered and in which he produced works of beauty, excitement, and significance.   He is the first American composer to have a critical edition of his complete works.

Guide to the Catalog

The Catalog of the Musical Works of William Billings is intended as a supplement to The Complete Works of William Billings, published by the American Musicological Society and The Colonial Society of Massachusetts in four volumes between 1977 and 1990. The Catalog supplies in a convenient format some of the information, such as source of the text, manuscript versions, and relationships between compositions, found in the Commentary section of each of the The Complete Works volumes. Additionally, it provides data not included in the Commentaries, such as the location of reprints and recordings of Billings's compositions and works of musical literature that discuss a composition.

The Catalog is divided between strophic pieces (primarily psalm- and fuging-tunes, plus several short set pieces) and anthems (usually through-composed settings of prose texts). The arrangement in the first section is alphabetical by tune title. The second section (the anthems) is arranged alphabetically by a text incipit. Although Billings sometimes gave names to his anthems, more often he simply called them "An Anthem," along with a note giving either the biblical chapter supplying the text or the occasion for which the anthem was written (e.g., "for Fast Day," "for Thanksgiving," &c.). Since anthems are usually identified by the first words of their text, this method seems most useful for the catalog.

The numbering of the pieces is sequential throughout the catalog.

In the strophic section, the following information is provided:

1) The Tunename is the primary identifier of a tune, and it rarely changed when a tune was reprinted. Occasionally, Billings supplied an alternate tunename (e.g., AN HYMN FOR CHRISTMAS and CHARLESTON). Alternate tunenames are given in the Notes section.

2) The Location supplies the first printing of the tune. In most cases, this occurred in one of Billings's own tunebooks, but a few tunes were published by others, either before Billings printed them, or they were never printed by Billings. The location gives the tunebook title and page number of the first printing, as well as the volume and page number for the work in The Complete Works edition.

3) The Source of Text gives the author of the words, along with the collection from which Billings may have taken the text. In some cases, when only the poet's name is given, the text was widely reprinted and its exact source is uncertain. In The New-England Psalm-Singer and Music in Miniature Billings published pieces without text, which are here designated as "Textless." However, in The New-England Psalm-Singer, Billings occasionally offered some suggested texts (e.g., "Psalm 148," or "Hymn 26"), without actually setting any words. These have been included in parentheses and are mentioned in the Notes section. Following the text source is the poetic Meter the tune is intended to accommodate. (LM is Long Meter, CM is Common Meter, SM is Short Meter, HM is Hallelujah Meter; PM -- Particular Meter -- is always followed by the number of syllables per line and the number of lines constituting a stanza.) The last item in this section is the First Line of the text. For textless tunes, this item is omitted. Texts supplied by the editors of The Complete Works volumes are not included in this catalog. However, when Billings suggests a text in The New-England Psalm-Singer, a text incipit is given in the first-line position.

4) Technical data on the tune are supplied next. Under Tune Type, the various formal schemes of Billings's tunes are given. A Plain Tune is one which sets a single verse of text

syllabically, without any musical elaboration of that text (such as repeated words, melismas, &c.). A Tune With Extension (abbreviated Twx) is a setting whose formal scheme does not depend entirely upon the text, but which, through word repetition, melismas, or setting of more than one stanza, extends the length of the tune beyond that of a single-stanza, syllabic setting. Antiphonal tunes have at least one phrase with reduced vocal scoring, in which one or more voices are silent. Both Plain Tunes and Tunes With Extension may be Antiphonal.

A Fuging Tune is a psalm-tune which usually includes at least one section with imitative or quasi-imitative counterpoint. Normally, a fuging tune has a well defined formal structure: the first part is chordal, coming to a distinct cadence; the second part begins with a motive (more often rhythmic than melodic) in one voice that is then taken up successively by the other voices, causing different words to be sung simultaneously in the various parts. This verbal conflict is a distinguishing feature of the fuging-tune. Fuging tunes are of two basic types: one includes a fuge that is an optional contrapuntal section, which may be sung or not at the discretion of the performers without affecting the completeness and utility of the psalm-tune. This type is designated as Fuging Chorus in the catalog. A second type has a fugal section that is an integral part of the tune's structure, without which it would be incomplete. This type is simply called a Fuging Tune in the catalog.

A Set Piece is usually a through-composed setting of a poetical text, made so that the substitution of other words is either inappropriate or impossible. Billings, however, made through-composed settings of poetry that he called anthems, and he frequently intermingled verse and Biblical prose in his anthems. In the catalog, those tunes are designated Set Piece when they are short enough to be strophic pieces (setting no more than three or four stanzas), but their tune structure is devised in such a way as to make text substitution unlikely. Those settings of poetry which Billings called anthems are included in the second section.

Following the tune type is a count of the <u>Number of Measures</u> in the tune, the <u>Key</u>, the <u>Time Signature</u> or signatures used in the piece, and an <u>Incipit</u>, a numerical representation of the first thirteen pitches of the melody. The measure count is based on Billings's own printing, and differences between that and the Complete Works edition, the result of rebarring some pieces, are given in parentheses. The key is designated by its letter name and indicated as major or minor by either capital or lower-case letters respectively. In most cases, the time signature is given as it appears in Billings's own scores; however, following the practice of The Complete Works, the reversed C symbol, designating the third mood of Common Time, is not used and 2/2 is substituted. Similarly, the C symbol with a vertical line through it, designating the second mood of Common Time, is indicated by the time signature 4/4. All changes of time signature in a tune are given, but users of the catalog are referred to the music for their precise location.

The thirteen-digit incipit is a numerical representation of the melody of the tune, omitting rests, rhythms, and octave transpositions. Thirteen pitches are usually sufficient to differentiate one tune from another in psalmody. The number 1 designates the first scale degree, whether major or minor, and the numbers 2 through 7 are successively the second through seventh scalar pitches. Accidental sharps and flats are ignored. The principal melody in Billings's music is normally found in the tenor voice, and it is understood that the incipit refers to this part unless otherwise indicated. Occasionally, in some Antiphonal Tunes, Billings begins with another part, or the tenor may start the melody but drop out for a few measures before the incipit is complete. These changes in voice are designated by the letters S:, A:, T:, B: (standing for Soprano, Alto, Tenor, and Bass) before the numbers at the point of shift.

5) Reprints of Billings's tunes were common throughout the years between 1770 and 1820, the psalmody era in American music. The catalog attempts to locate reprints of Billings's tunes in various tunebooks published in America during those years. The listing is based on the Early American Imprints microcards published by the Readex Corporation and prepared by the American Antiquarian Society. The microcards are arranged by the numbers given in the Charles Evans and Shaw-Shoemaker catalogs of early American imprints. In the listing of tunebooks cited, the Evans or Shaw-Shoemaker number for an

item is given in square brackets following the citation. A few rare tunebooks are not included in the Evans and Shaw-Shoemaker bibliographies. Citations and listings of Billings's tunes were taken from microfilm copies of those tunebooks in the compiler's possession. The listing attempts to be comprehensive, but not exhaustive.

The tunebook containing the reprint is identified by a number in boldface type. The tunebooks represented by these numbers can be found in the "List of Works Cited." The tunebook identifier is followed by the page in the book on which the Billings work is found. If the reprint is essentially the same as Billings published the piece, only the page number is given; if, however, there is some significant alteration in the music, the notation "(v)" follows the page number. Some reprints of Billings's tunes in British tunebooks have also been located, but no attempt has been made to be comprehensive. These reprints are given in the Notes section, and sigla for these tunebooks can also be found in the "List of Works Cited."

6) Manuscripts. Billings's music in manuscript copy has been located and identified. Not every Billings work in manuscript is significant; many are merely copies of published pieces, some dating perhaps from the early years of the nineteenth century. Others, however, contain pieces that Billings never published, or variant versions of tunes, sometimes with sections that Billings did not include in his published versions. The manuscripts listed in this section are those which contain early or variant versions of Billings's pieces, which seem to cast light upon Billings's development as a composer, or which exemplify the manuscript transmission of his music. The locations of the manuscripts copies, most of which are supplements to other tunebooks, are given in National Union Catalog symbols. These symbols are identified in the "List of Works Cited" section.

7) The Notes section contains miscellaneous information about the piece which seems important for the user to know. It is often used to draw attention to relationships between Billings's compositions or to point out significant technical features in a particular work.

8) The Literature section contains citations to works where information about or significant discussions of the

piece can be found. The work is identified by the last name of the author, followed by the first initials of the title of the book or article if needed to differentiate between several works by the same writer. The page on which the discussion takes place is next given. If the page number is followed by "(f)", this indicates that a facsimile of the piece is printed in the work. Bibliographic citations for these works can also be found in the "List of Works Cited."

9) Recordings of Billings works have been located for those which are performed essentially as he wrote them, i.e., as choral music. Only commercially released recordings have been included; non-commercial and private recordings have been omitted. Instrumental arrangements and performances as solo works with accompaniment have not been included. The discographic citations are listed in the "List of Works Cited."

The information given for anthems is largely the same as that given for psalm- and fuging-tunes. However, a few extra items are included and some are omitted, as follows:

1) As noted above, the anthems are entered alphabetically by their text incipit, therefore an entry is made for the actual title that Billings gave to the work. These can be found through the " Anthem Title Index."

2) Since anthems are not metered, and the anthem is identified by the first line of text, those items are omitted from the Source of text section. This section includes, so far as possible, all Biblical and other text sources that have been identified for a Billings work.

3) In the technical information section, since these are all anthems or anthem-like works, Tune type has been omitted. Under Time Sig. the time signatures of the major sections of the anthem are given. If the section frequently changes time signature but the musical flow is continuous, a notation such as "3/2 and 2/2 intermixed" is used. As with psalm- and fuging-tunes, the reversed C time signature is represented by 2/2 and the C with a slash by 4/4. Since anthems sometimes change tempo between sections, the location of all Directive Words in a piece is given. Finally, since anthems are works of some length, it may be useful to know the approximate Timing of a piece. This has been arrived at by totaling the number of measures in a particular time signature, then

calculating the duration of the music in that time signature by using the standard metronomic equivalents for the tempo indicated by the signature. The timings include all repetitions of sections, and the effect of any directive words on the tempo is considered in accordance with Billings's instructions in the "Dialogue" section of The Continental Harmony. There Billings said that directive words make a difference of "one quarter part quicker or slower." Timings, of course, are approximate. We do not know how precisely Federal Era singers adhered to the recommended tempi for the time signatures. However, even an approximate timing should be useful to the researcher and performer.

The "List of Works Cited" includes citations for American and British tunebooks, books and articles, manuscripts, and sound recordings referred to in the catalog. The American tunebooks are arranged alphabetically by compiler, except for Billings's works, which are listed by the widely accepted abbreviations for their titles: NEPS for The New-England Psalm-Singer, SMA for Singing Master's Assistant, MIM for Music in Miniature, PSA for The Psalm-Singer's Amusement, and CH for The Continental Harmony. Abbreviations for the tunebooks, which may occasionally be used in the catalog, are given preceding the citation. The numbers preceding American tunebook citations are referred to in the reprints section of the catalog entries. The recordings are arranged generally in reverse chronological order and are referenced by the capital letter preceding the citation.

At the end are five indexes. The "First Line Index" presents in an alphabetical arrangement the texts listed under each catalog entry. If a tune is described only as "Textless," no entry appears in the First Line Index. The "Anthem Title Index" is an alphabetical listing of anthem titles that Billings used. The " Text Source Index" lists alphabetically under the name of the poet or title of the text source the sources from which Billings drew his texts. For Biblical books, only the name of the book is listed, not the specific chapter and verse. The works that use this text are then listed to the right in alphabetical order. An "Tune Type Index" identifies the form or type of tune represented by each of Billings's compositions (except anthems). The type of tune is listed alphabetically in the left column; the tunes which correspond to this type are given alphabetically in the right column. Finally, the "Incipit Index" is a numerical arrangement of the incipit listings.

The arrangements of ten British psalm tunes published in Music in Miniature have not been included in this catalog.

Catalog
of the
Musical Works
of
William Billings

Billings Works Catalog

PSALM- AND HYMN-TUNES

1. ADAMS

  Location: Continental Harmony, p.153
         Complete Works: IV, p.228
  Source of text: Watts, Psalm 84, v.5   Meter: HM
    First line: To spend one sacred day
  Tune type: Twx   No. of measures: 14 Key: C
    Time Sig.: 6/4   Incipit: 1176517115171
  Reprints by Billings: None   Reprints by others: None

2. ADORATION

  Location: Psalm-Singers Amusement, p.79-81
         Complete Works: III, p.109
  Source of text: Watts, Hymns III, No.32   Meter: LM
    First line: To God the Father, God the Son
  Tune type: Fuging chorus No. of measures: 51   Key: D
    Time Sig.: 3/2; 3/4 Incipit: 5343456567156
  Reprints by Billings: None   Reprints by others: None

3. AFRICA

Location: New-England Psalm-Singer, p.14
        Complete Works: I, p.88, II, p.46
Source of text: NEPS: Textless; SMA: Watts, Hymns I,
    No.39   Meter: CM First line: SMA: Now shall my inward
    joy arise
Tune type: Plain No. of measures: 14   Key: E-flat
    Time Sig.: 3/2 Incipit: 1345176513432
Reprints by Billings: **146** 4(rev); **111** 21(rev)
    Reprints by others: **10** 13, **22** 71, **36** 18, **62** 7, **63** 107,
    64 68, **65** 62, **66** 15, **68** 391(diff. text), **89** 31, **103**
    45(in D major), **104** 18, **135** 33, **143** 31, **152** 105, **153**
    105, **154** 105, **155** 80, **156** 80, **157** 80, **158** 80, **170** 68,
    171 62, **172** 15, **173** 116, **180** 111
Literature: BarbourCM 84, MacDougall 67(f)
Recordings: A

4. ALBANY

Location: New-England Psalm-Singer, p.17
        Complete Works: I, p.98
Source of text: Textless   Meter: CM
Tune type: Plain No. of measures: 14   Key: a
    Time Sig.: 3/2   Incipit: 1151345132112
Reprints by Billings: None   Reprints by others: None

5. AMERICA

Location: New-England Psalm-Singer, p.7
        Complete Works: I, p.40; II, p.50
Source of text: NEPS: Mather Byles; SMA: Billings
    Meter: PM [8.8.8.8.8.8]   First line: NEPS: To thee
    the tuneful anthem soars; SMA: Come let us sing unto
    the Lord
Tune type: Plain No. of measures: 24   Key: D
    Time Sig.: 3/2   Incipit: NEPS: 1154317176555;
    SMA: 5543171765554
Reprints by Billings: **146** 5(v); **111** 21(v)

Reprints by others: **15** 39, **16** 77, **80** 19, **149** 177, **136**
95, **166** 58, **167** 59, **168** 48, **169** 46
Manuscripts: CtY Ms, MSaE Ms2, MWA Ms
Literature: WienandtBC 28

6. AMHERST

Location: New-England Psalm-Singer, p.48
          Complete Works: I, p.182, II, p.54
Source of text: Brady & Tate, Psalm 136   Meter: HM
   First line: To God, the mighty Lord
Tune type: Twx No of measures: NEPS: 13; SMA: 18
   Key: G Time Sig.: NEPS: 3/2; SMA: 2/2
   Incipit: NEPS: 1354215156543; SMA:1354321515654
Reprints by Billings: **146** 7; **111** 11   Reprints by others:
   1 21, **2** 21, **3** 21, **4** 41, **5** 41, **6** 41, **7** 21, **8** 55, **10** 12,
   18 107, **22** 91, **32** 24, **33** 24, **36** 56, **46** 90, **48** 126, **49**
   56, **50** 67, **60** 76, **73** 18, **80** 27, **85** 215(v), **87** 18(**112**
   ver), **89** 30, **103** 117, **104** 47, **105** 48, **106** 12(**112** ver.),
   110 17, **113** 12, **117** 13, **118** 10, **119** 106, **131** 101, **132**
   77, **145** 29, **136** 12(**112** ver), **137** 29, **138** 17, **139** 71,
   140 22, **141** 56, **150** 43, **151** 43, **152** 47, **153** 47, **154** 47,
   155 38, **156** 38, **157** 38, **158** 38, **159** 38, **160** 38, **161** 38,
   162 38, **163** 38, **164** 38, **166** 54, **167** 54, **168** 44, **169** 41,
   170 21, **171** 22, **172** 105, **173** 48, **176** 32, **177** 32, **178**
   60, **179** 60
Manuscripts: MSaE Ms2
Literature: CrawfordCR xxiii

7. ANDOVER

Location: New-England Psalm-Singer, p.65
          Complete Works: I, p.234
Source of text: Textless   Meter: CM
Tune type: Plain No. of measures: 14   Key: C
   Time Sig.: 3/2 Incipit: 1521432154322
Reprints by Billings: None   Reprints by others: None

8. ANDOVER

Location: Psalm-Singer's Amusement, p.78
          Complete Works: III, p.105
Source of text: Watts, Hymns I, No.20   Meter: CM
    First line: Awake, my heart, arise, my tongue
Tune type: Fuging chorus   No. of measures: 34   Key: D
    Time Sig.: 3/2; 2/2   Incipit: 5171765671271
Reprints by Billings: None   Reprints by others: None

9. ASHFORD

Location: New-England Psalm-Singer, p.89
          Complete Works: I, p.314
Source of text: Brady & Tate, Psalm 23   Meter: CM
    First line: The Lord himself, the mighty Lord
Tune type: Antiphonal verse & chorus
    No. of measures: 19 (24)   Key: C   Time Sig.: 3/2
    Incipit: 1176543454321
Reprints by Billings: None   Reprints by others: None
Literature: BarbourCM 35

10. ASHHAM

Location: Singing Master's Assistant, p.40
          Complete Works: II, p.150, III, p.278
Source of text: Watts, Hymns I, No.67   Meter: LM
    First line: Thou whom my soul admires above
Tune type: Plain   No. of measures: 8   Key: A
    Time Sig.: 6/8   Incipit: 1123212171232
Reprints by Billings: None   Reprints by others: 55
    9(var. as Lesson VIII), 135 28(var. as Lesson VIII)

11. ASIA

Location: New-England Psalm-Singer, p.60
          Complete Works: I, p.214
Source of text: Textless   Meter: SM
Tune type: Plain   No. of measures: 14   Key: a
    Time Sig.: C   Incipit: 1234322334455
Reprints by Billings: None   Reprints by others: None

Notes: COBHAM (**31** 185) is a possible variant

12. ASIA

Location: Music In Miniature, p.26
        Complete Works: II, p.304
Source of text: Textless   Meter: SM
Tune type: Plain No. of measures: 14 Key: A
    Time Sig.: 2/2 Incipit: 1343543212321
Reprints by Billings: None   Reprints by others: None
Notes: LIBERTY (**112** 9) is a possible earlier version
Literature: KroegerWBM 343

13. ASSURANCE

Location: Psalm-Singer's Amusement, p.8
        Complete Works, III, p.14
Source of text: Watts, Psalm 27, v.5   Meter: CM
    First line: Now shall my head be lifted high
Tune type: Double fuging-tune No. of measures: 15
    Key: A   Time Sig.: 6/4 Incipit: 1333213555567
Reprints by Billings: None   Reprints by others: **36** 174,
    145 149(v), **168** 128(v), **169** 108(v)
Manuscripts: MiU-C Ms2 105 (Bass voice only)
Notes: Changes in **168** version may have been made by
    Billings himself.
Recordings: Y

14. ATTLEBOROUGH

Location: New-England Psalm-Singer, p.59
        Complete Works, I, p.210
Source of text: Textless   Meter: SM
Tune type: Plain No. of measures: 13 Key: F
    Time Sig.: 3/2 Incipit: 1565432343215
Reprints by Billings: None   Reprints by others: None
Notes: Billings's title spelled ATTLEOBROUGH

15. AURORA

Location: Singing Master's Assistant, p.1

Complete Works, II, p.37
Source of text: Billings   Meter: SM
  First line: Awake, my soul, awake
Tune type: Fuging chorus No. of measures: 24   Key: C
  Time Sig.: 3/2; 2/2 Incipit: 5135432123217
Reprints by Billings: **111** 11(fuge omitted)
  Reprints by others: **7** 70(fuge omitted, called MORNING),
  15 40, **22** 46, **26** 29, **27** 29, **28** 29, **36** 175, **81** 19, **103**
  78(fuge omitted), **119** 78(v), **135** 38, **136** 91, **166** 64,
  167 64
Notes: DICKINSON (**112** 73) is a possible variant. Following
  tunename is the note "a Morning Hymn."
Literature: NathanWB 29(f)

16. BALTIMORE

Location: Singing Master's Assistant, p.47
         Complete Works: II, p.165
Source of text: Billings   Meter: PM [5656664]
  First line: Father of mercies
Tune type: Twx   No. of measures: 9 Key: C
  Time Sig.: 6/4   Incipit: 1111332721432
Reprints by Billings: None   Reprints by others: **52** 94(v),
  53 94(v), **119** 220(v)
Literature: BarbourCM 48

17. BAPTISM

Location: Suffolk Harmony, p.37
         Complete Works: III, p.188
Source of text: James Relly, Christian Hymns, Hymn 11
  Meter: PM [887887224448]   First line: O how doth God
  our souls surprise
Tune type: Twx verse and chorus   No. of measures: 25
  Key: d Time Sig.: 6/4; 2/4   Incipit: 5543711765564
Reprints by Billings: None   Reprints by others: None
Literature: McKay 148(f)

18. BARRE

Location: New-England Psalm-Singer, p.67
          Complete Works: I, p.243; III, p.280
Source of text: Textless   Meter: CM
Tune type: Plain No. of measures: 15 Key: G
   Time Sig.: 2/4 Incipit: 1515143215176
Reprints by Billings: None   Reprints by others: 55 12(as
   BARRY, var., Text: Watts, Divine Songs, No.1)
Notes: The title is probably a reference to Col. Isaac
   Barrė, a champion of the rights of the American
   colonies in the British parliament.
Literature: Schrader 426

19. BEDFORD

Location: Sacred Harmony (1788), p.98
          Complete Works: III, p.281
Source of text: Watts, Hymns I, No.64   Meter: SM
   First line: Behold, what wondrous grace
Tune type: Plain No. of measures: 14 Key: A
   Time Sig.: 3/4 Incipit: 5123212343221
Reprints by Billings: None   Reprints by others: None
Notes: Ascribed to Billings on the basis of its being a
   variant of WALTHAM (146 20).

20. BELLINGHAM

Location: Continental Harmony, p.58
          Complete Works: IV, p.78
Source of text: Watts, Hymns II, No.69   Meter: CM
   First line: Begin, my tongue, some heav'nly theme
Tune type: Antiphonal Twx No. of measures: 27
   Key: E-flat Time Sig.: 3/2; 2/2 Incipit: 5156517116517
Reprints by Billings: None   Reprints by others: None

21. BENEFICENCE

Location: Suffolk Harmony, p.10
          Complete Works: III, p.150
Source of text: Brady & Tate, Psalm 112   Meter: LM

First line: That man is blest who stands in awe
Tune type: Antiphonal verse and chorus
No. of measures: 17 Key: C Time Sig.: 2/2; 6/4
Incipit: 5111234321221
Reprints by Billings: None   Reprints by others: None
Notes: following title: Suitable for a Charity meeting.
Literature: BarbourCM 113

22. BENEVOLENCE

Location: Singing Master's Assistant, p.72
          Complete Works: II, p.213
Source of text: Brady & Tate, Psalm 41   Meter: CM
    First line: Happy the man whose tender care
Tune type: Fuging tune   No. of measures: 29 Key: F
    Time Sig.: 2/2   Incipit: 1123215554343
Reprints by Billings: None   Reprints by others: **75** 137(v)
Notes: The fuging section follows without a break in the
    musical flow.

23. BENNINGTON

Location: Waterhouse Ms, p.12
          Complete Works: III, p.312
Source of text: Watts, Horae Lyricae, "The Nativity of
    Christ" Meter: CM First line: Shepherds rejoice,
    lift up your eyes
Tune type: Plain No. of measures: 14 Key: G
    Time Sig.: 3/2 Incipit: 1321321222343
Reprints by Billings: None   Reprints by others: None
Manuscripts: MiU-C Ms2 114
Notes: Ascribed to Billings on the basis of its being a
    variant of FRIENDSHIP (**112** 61).
Literature: KroegerWBM 339

24. BERLIN

Location: Psalm-Singer's Amusement, p.3
          Complete Works: III, p.5

Source of text: Watts, Horae Lyricae, "Christ Dying,
   Rising and Reigning," v.1-2 Meter: LM First line: He
   dies! the heav'nly lover dies
Tune type: Set Piece No. of measures: 46 Key: e
   Time Sig.: 2/2; 3/2; 2/4 Incipit: 5517534543215
Reprints by Billings: None   Reprints by others: 15 60, 22
   40(v), 32 82, 33 82, 46 75, 81 14(v), 82 46(v), 89
   44(v), 136 75(v), 138 38(v), 145 130(v), 155 221, 156
   221, 157 221, 158 221, 166 67(v), 167 67(v), 168 52(v),
   169 50(v), 170 59(v)
Literature: BarbourBB 46; NathanWB 33(f)

25. BETHLEHEM

Location: Singing Master's Assistant, p.69
           Complete Works: II, p.207
Source of text: Brady & Tate, Supplement, Hymn 11
   Meter: CM First line: While shepherds watch their
   flocks by night
Tune type: Fuging chorus No. of measures: 31 Key: E
   Time Sig.: 3/2; 2/2; 3/2 Incipit: 5171765434321
Reprints by Billings: 111 17 (fuge omitted)
   Reprints by others: 4 102, 5 102, 6 102, 16 129, 21
   49, 22 20(111 ver), 80 52, 82 28(v), 85 59, 106 28, 135
   42, 136 28, 137 62(v), 140 1, 141 17, 145 62(v), 166
   40, 167 39, 168 34(v), 169 34(v), 170 24, 171 24, 180
   124
Notes: Billings erroneously attributes the text to Watts.
Literature: BarbourCM 116; KroegerST 27
Recordings: C, AG

26. BIRD, THE

Location: Independent publication (1790)
           Complete Works: III, p.225
Source of text: Brady & Tate, Psalm 11   Meter: CM
   First line: Since I have plac'd my trust in God
Tune type: Fuging chorus No. of measures: 33 Key: g
   Time Sig.: 3/2; 2/2; 3/2; 2/2 Incipit: 1543234351432

Reprints by Billings: None   Reprints by others: **122**
(paged sep. at end)
Manuscripts: NN Ms, T & B only, first 14 m. missing, many
differences in pitch and rhythm; Ms. possibly dates
from 1773.
Notes: Bound with some copies of **144**.
Literature: WienandtBC 56
Recordings: D, R, AF

27. BOLTON

Location: Singing Master's Assistant, p.25
          Complete Works: II, p.116
Source of text: Charles Wesley, from Whitefield,
    Collection, Hymn 20   Meter: HM   First line: Rejoice,
    the Lord is king
Tune type: Antiphonal Twx   No. of measures: 17   Key: G
    Time Sig.: 6/8   Incipit: 1171235443143
Reprints by Billings: None   Reprints by others: None
Manuscripts: a variant version called SPENCER in
      Waterhouse Ms, p.7.
Notes: Billings attributes the text to G. Whitefield.
Literature: KroegerWBM 339

28. BOSTON

Location: New-England Psalm-Singer, p.23
          Complete Works: I, p.120, II, p.40
Source of text: NEPS: Watts, Horae Lyricae, "The Nativity
    of Christ"; SMA: Billings   Meter: CM First line:
    NEPS: Shepherds rejoice, lift up your eyes;
    SMA: Methinks I see a heav'nly host
Tune type: Twx   No. of measures: 18   Key: B-flat
    Time Sig.: 2/2   Incipit: 1555517655123
Reprints by Billings: **146** 2(v)   Reprints by others: **36**
    153, **81** 22, **82** 17, **84** 32, **119** 17, **124** 76, **125** 52, **135**
    45, **140** 38, **141** 50, **180** 35
Notes: In **112** Billings identifies the text as "Hymn

33d." (i.e., Hymn 33 in <u>Appendix</u>. Title followed by
note: for Christmas. Same text used for first 2
stanzas of SHILOH (**144** 1)
<u>Literature</u>: BarbourCM 44; Stevenson 64
<u>Recordings</u>: B, C, N, AS

29. BRADFORD

<u>Location</u>: Waterhouse Ms, p.15
        Complete Works: III, p.314
<u>Source of text</u>: Watts, Psalm 47   <u>Meter</u>: CM
    <u>First line</u>: O for a shout of sacred joy
<u>Tune type</u>: Twx verse and chorus   <u>No. of measures</u>: 20
    <u>Key:</u> E   <u>Time Sig.</u>: 3/2; 6/4   <u>Incipit</u>: 5543432123455
<u>Reprints by Billings</u>: None   <u>Reprints by others</u>: None
<u>Notes</u>: Ascribed to Billings on the basis of its being a
    variant version of CONSOLATION (**146** 19).
<u>Literature</u>: KroegerWBM 340

30. BRAINTREE

<u>Location</u>: New-England Psalm-Singer, p.43
        Complete Works: I, p.164
<u>Source of text</u>: Textless   <u>Meter</u>: PM [888888]
<u>Tune type</u>: Plain   <u>No. of measures</u>: 25 <u>Key:</u> D
    <u>Time Sig.</u>: C   <u>Incipit</u>: 5534564551765
<u>Reprints by Billings</u>: None   <u>Reprints by others</u>: None
<u>Notes</u>: Billings's title spelled "BRANETREE."

31. BRATTLE SQUARE

<u>Location</u>: Suffolk Harmony, p.10
        Complete Works: III, p.148
<u>Source of text</u>: Watts, Hymns I, No.62   <u>Meter</u>: CM
    <u>First line</u>: Come let us join our cheerful songs
<u>Tune type</u>: Plain   <u>No. of measures</u>: 14   <u>Key:</u> D
    <u>Time Sig.</u>: 3/2   <u>Incipit</u>: 5345671767512
<u>Reprints by Billings</u>: None   <u>Reprints by others</u>: None

32. BRATTLE STREET

Location: New-England Psalm-Singer, p.19
          Complete Works: I, p.107
Source of text: Textless   Meter: LM
Tune type: Twx No. of measures: 32 Key: G
    Time Sig.: 3/2 Incipit: 1345171654556
Reprints by Billings: None   Reprints by others: None
Manuscripts: Waterhouse Ms 11 (ends after 16 measures),
    MiU-C Ms2 (ends after 16 measures)

33. BRATTLE STREET

Location: Suffolk Harmony, p.19
          Complete Works: III, p.161
Source of text: Watts, Psalm 92, Pt.1   Meter: LM
    First line: Sweet is the work my God, my king
Tune type: Fuging chorus No. of measures: 30 Key: A
    Time Sig.: 3/2 Incipit: 1321234553432
Reprints by Billings: None   Reprints by others: None
Notes: a possible variant of BREST (111 4)
Literature: KroegerWBM 342

34. BREST

Location: Music in Miniature, p.4
          Complete Works: II, p.280
Source of text: Textless   Meter: LM
Tune type: Plain No. of measures: 17 Key: A
    Time Sig.: 4/4 Incipit: 1123543211235
Reprints by Billings: None   Reprints by others: None
Notes: BRATTLE STREET (144 19) is a possible variant.
Literature: KroegerWBM 342

35. BRIDGWATER

Location: New-England Psalm-Singer, p.40
          Complete Works: I, p.154
Source of text: Billings   Meter: LM
    First line: Majestyck God, when I descry
Tune type: Plain No. of measures: 16 Key: F

Time Sig.: 3/2 Incipit: 1565165671117
Reprints by Billings: None   Reprints by others: None
Notes: Same text used for SUNDAY (146 54). Alternate
    title: EVENING HYMN.

36. BROAD COVE

Location: Continental Harmony, p.129
          Complete Works: IV, p.191
Source of text: Watts, Hymns II, No.58   Meter: CM
    First line: Time, what an empty vapor 'tis
Tune type: Fuging tune   No. of measures: 26 Key: g
    Time Sig.: 3/2; 2/2 Incipit: 1553455432135
Reprints by Billings: None   Reprints by others: None

37. BROOKFIELD

Location: New-England Psalm-Singer, p.7
          Complete Works: I, p.64, II, p.48
Source of text: NEPS: Textless (Watts, Hyms III, No.1);
    SMA: Watts, Hymns III, No.1 Meter: LM
    First line: 'Twas on that dark, that doleful night
Tune type: Plain   No. of measures: 16 Key: d
    Time Sig.: 3/2 Incipit: 5132321712232
Reprints by Billings: 146 4, 111 22   Reprints by others:
    1 6, 2 6, 3 6, 4 26, 5 26, 6 26, 8 41, 10 16, 11 15, 12
    15, 13 15, 14 12, 15 10, 21 59, 22 111, 25 27, 29 21,
    30 26(v), 36 24, 40 27(v), 46 25, 48 121, 49 94, 50
    128, 58 60, 60 50, 63 105, 68 425(v), 73 17, 74 73, 78
    29, 79 34, 80 4, 82 4, 86 32, 87 18(112 ver), 89 45, 92
    51, 93 51, 94 51, 95 51, 96 47, 97 47, 98 47, 99 47,
    100 47, 101 47, 102 51, 106 25(112 ver), 113 59, 114
    15, 115 3(112 ver), 117 18, 118 13, 119 73, 120 72, 127
    57, 128 57, 133 36, 138 20, 139 28, 136 25, 137 39, 140
    45, 141 61, 143 40, 145 39, 149 81(112 ver), 150 83(v),
    151 83, 152 83(v), 153 83, 154 83(v), 155 68, 156 68,
    157 68, 158 68, 159 68, 160 68, 161 68, 162 68, 163 68,
    165 68, 166 36, 167 36, 168 30, 169 31, 176 27, 177
    43, 178 57, 179 57

Manuscripts: CtHT-W Ms, CtY Ms, DLC Ms (Billings
    autograph), NN Ms, RPB Ms
Notes: Although textless in NEPS, Billings suggests as a
    text source "Hymn 72d." (i.e. Hymn 72 in Appendix),
    which is Watts, Hymns III, No.1.
Literature: AndersonE 49(f); CrawfordCR xxviii; CrawfordMM
    586(f); Hamm 144; MacDougall 66(f);NathanWB 21(f)

38. BROOKLINE

Location: New-England Psalm-Singer, p.2
            Complete Works: I, p.42; II, p.300
Source of text: Textless (Brady & Tate, Psalm 19)
    Meter: CM First line: The heav'ns declare thy glory,
    Lord
Tune type: Plain   No. of measures: NEPS: 14; MIM: 15
    Key: A   Time Sig.: 2/2 Incipit: NEPS:1121712321434;
    MIM: 1121712321234
Reprints by Billings: 111 7(v) Reprints by others: 22 18
Notes: Although textless in 112, Billings suggests as a
    text source "Ps.19" (referring to Brady and Tate, New
    Version).

39. BRUNSWICK

Location: Singing Master's Assistant, p.8
            Complete Works: II, p.57
Source of text: Watts, Hymns II, No.28   Meter: CM
    First line: Stoop down my thoughts that use to rise
Tune type: Twx   No. of measures: 26 Key: f-sharp
    Time Sig.: 2/2   Incipit: 5123212323455
Reprints by Billings: None   Reprints by others: None

40. BURLINGTON

Location: Suffolk Harmony, p.49
            Complete Works: III, p.210
Source of text: James Relly, Christian Hymns, Hymn 3
    Meter: PM [76767876]   First line: Canaan promis'd is
    before
Tune type: Antiphonal Twx   No. of measures: 31

Key: B-flat   Time Sig.: 2/4 Incipit: 1155171S:132343
Reprints by Billings: None   Reprints by others: None

41. CALVARY

Location: Music in Miniature, p.29
         Complete Works: II, p.319
Source of text: Textless   Meter: CM
Tune type: Plain No. of measures: 14 Key: c
   Time Sig.: 3/2 Incipit: 5171235432115
Reprints by Billings: as first section of ST. THOMAS in 31
   127   Reprints by others: None

42. CAMBRIDGE

Location: New-England Psalm-Singer, p.47
         Complete Works: I, p.178; II, p.75
Source of text: NEPS: Textless; SMA: Watts, Psalm 113
   Meter: PM [888888] First line: SMA: Ye that delight to
   serve the Lord
Tune type: Plain No. of measures: 30 Key: C
   Time Sig.: 2/2 Incipit: 1321543223451
Reprints by Billings: 146 13(v); 111 20(v)
   Reprints by others: None
Manuscripts: CtY Ms
Notes: In 146 Billings credits the words to "T&B" (Brady &
   Tate).
Literature: BarbourCM 123

43. CAMDEN

Location: Suffolk Harmony, p.14
         Complete Works: III, p.154
Source of text: Watts, Psalm 104, v.1, and Psalm 148, v.12
   Meter: LM First line: My soul, thy great creator
   praise; Chorus: Speak of wonders of that love
Tune type: Antiphonal verse and chorus
   No. of measures: 32 Key: E-flat Time Sig.: 6/4; 2/4
   Incipit: 15345671765A:56
Reprints by Billings: None   Reprints by others: None

44. CANON of 4 in 1, A

Location: New-England Psalm-Singer, p.46
         Complete Works: I, p.177
Source of text: Text.ess   Meter: LM
Tune type: Plain No. of measures: 16 Key: B-flat
   Time Sig.: 3/4 Incipit: 1335321711115
Reprints by Billings: None   Reprints by others: None

45. CANON of 4 in 1, A

Location: New-England Psalm-Singer, p.56
         Complete Works: I, p.203
Source of text: Perez Morton   Meter: LM
   First line: When Jesus wept, the falling tear
Tune type: Plain   No. of measures: 16 Key: f-sharp
   Time Sig.: 3/2 Incipit: 1545673543211
Reprints by Billings: None   Reprints by others: None
Notes: Same text used for EMMAUS (146 20)
Literature: Boroff 42(f); Chase 143; Kingman 133; Marrocco
   111
Recordings: J, K, N, P, Q, R, S, V, W, AL, AO

46. CANON of 4 in 1, A

Location: New-England Psalm-Singer, p.85
         Complete Works: I, p.303
Source of text: Watts, Hymns I, No.87   Meter: LM
   First line: Thus saith the high and lofty one
Tune type: Plain   No. of measures: 16 Key: G
   Time Sig.: 3/2   Incipit: 1321234543217
Reprints by Billings: None   Reprints by others: None
Literature: HitchcockMUS 11
Recordings: H

47. CANON of 6 in One with a Ground, A

Location: New-England Psalm-Singer, frontispiece
         Complete Works: I, p.39
Source of text: Mather Byles   Meter: PM [888888]
   First line: Wake ev'ry breath and ev'ry string

Tune type: Plain No. of measures: 24 Key: C
   Time Sig.: 3/2 Incipit: 1343212345432
Reprints by Billings: None   Reprints by others: None
Notes: the canon is engraved in circular form surrounding
      a picture.
Literature: CrawfordMM 586(f); Hamm 141(f); HitchcockWB
    55(f); Lawrence 47(f); NathanWB 18(f); Stevenson
    (f fig.7)

48. CHELSEA

Location: New-England Psalm-Singer, p.48
           Complete Works: I, p.180
Source of text: Textless   Meter: LM
Tune type: Plain No. of measures: 15 (16) Key: D
   Time Sig.: 3/2 Incipit: 5345671765435
Reprints by Billings: None   Reprints by others: None
Notes: title spelled CHELLSEA

49. CHELSEA

Location: Suffolk Harmony, p.48
           Complete Works: III, p.208
Source of text: James Relly, Christian Hymns, Hymn 43
   Meter: PM [5.5.11] First line: What beauties divine
Tune type: Antiphonal Plain   No. of measures: 8 Key: G
   Time Sig.: 6/4   Incipit: 5111123333517
Reprints by Billings: None   Reprints by others: None

50. CHESTER

Location: New-England Psalm-Singer, p.91
           Complete Works: I, p.321; II, p.72
Source of text: Billings   Meter: LM First line: Let
   tyrants shake their iron rod
Tune type: Plain   No. of measures: 16 Key: F
   Time Sig.: 2/2 Incipit: 5671561765555
Reprints by Billings: 146 12(v), 111 12(v)
   Reprints by others: 11 15, 12 15, 13 15, 22 111(111
   ver), 26 35(v), 27 35(v), 28 35(v), 36 89, 44 43, 46
   85, 48 130, 49 60, 52 41, 53 41, 62 7, 64 72, 65 64, 66

15, **67** 16, **80** 8, **86** 32, **87** 17, **104** 21, **107** 26, **114** 13,
118 71, **135** 50, **136** 85, **149** 43, **150** 91, **151** 91, **152** 91,
153 91, **154** 91, **155** 71, **156** 71, **157** 71, **158** 71, **166** 27,
167 25, **168** 23, **169** 22, **170** 29, **171** 25, **172** 15, **173** 60,
178 47, **179** 47

Manuscripts: CtY Ms, NYPL Ms

Notes: in **112** Billings supplies only the first verse of
the text. Billings's original patriotic text is seldom
found set to this tune in the reprints. Most often
Doddridge's Hymns, No.56, v.2 (Let the high heav'ns
your songs invite) is set.

Literature: AndersonE 54(f); Atkins 7; Boroff 420(f);
CrawfordCR xxx; CrawfordMAB 8, Kingman 131; Lawrence
81(f); Lindstrom 482(f); MacDougall 60(f); Marrocco
112; McKay 63

Recordings: S, U, Y, AH, AI, AM, AO, AP, AQ, AS, AT

51. CHESTERFIELD

Location: New-England Psalm-Singer, p.63
          Complete Works: I, p.224
Source of text: Textless   Meter: CM
Tune type: Plain   No. of measures: 14 Key: d
    Time Sig.: 3/2 Incipit: 1513153511765
Reprints by Billings: None   Reprints by others: None
Literature: BarbourCM 121
Recordings: E

52. CHOCKSETT

Location: Singing Master's Assistant, p.49
          Complete Works: II, p.168
Source of text: Watts, Psalm 84   Meter: HM
    First line: Lord of the worlds above
Tune type: Twx   No. of measures: 18 Key: G
    Time Sig.: 2/2 Incipit: 1123454323432
Reprints by Billings: **111** 10   Reprints by others: **22** 39,
    44 48
Manuscripts: NN Ms2 8

53. CLAREMONT

Location: Continental Harmony, p.154
          Complete Works: IV, p.230
Source of text: Anon, text in Tans'ur RMC, p.152
   Meter: PM [886886] First line: Arise and hail the
   sacred day
Tune type: Twx   No. of measures: 17 Key: C
   Time Sig.: 6/8 Incipit: 5123132171512
Reprints by Billings: None   Reprints by others: None
Notes: Caption title on music spelled CLARIMONT (corrected
   in index). Title followed by the note "A Hymn for
   Easter."

54. COBHAM

Location: Continental Harmony, p.185
          Complete Works: IV, p.276
Source of text: Watts, Psalm 39, Pt.2, v.1-2   Meter: CM
   First line: Teach me the measure of my days
Tune type: Antiphonal Twx   No. of measures: 19 Key: a
   Time Sig.: 6/8 Incipit: 1123543223123
Reprints by Billings: None   Reprints by others: None
Manuscripts: Waterhouse Ms 13, called RAYNHAM, T & B parts
   only, follows a piece dated 16 March 1781; MiU-C Ms2
   109, called RAYNHAM, T & B parts only.
Notes: First half of tune is a variant of ASIA (112 60).
Literature: KroegerWBM 343
Recordings: R

55. COHASSET

Location: Continental Harmony, p.59
          Complete Works: IV, p.80
Source of text: Watts, Hymns I, No.88   Meter: LM
   First line: Life is the time to serve the Lord
Tune type: Fuging chorus   No. of measures: 27 Key: a
   Time Sig.: 3/2; 2/2 Incipit: 1321234513217
Reprints by Billings: None   Reprints by others: None

56. COLUMBIA

Location: Singing Master's Assistant, p.56
         Complete Works: II, p.182
Source of text: Billings   Meter: HM   First line: Not
   all the pow'rs on earth
Tune type: Twx   No. of measures: 18 Key: E
   Time Sig.: 2/2 Incipit: 5316715314325
Reprints by Billings: 111 14   Reprints by others: 15 63,
   22 3ɔ, 26 32, 27 32, 28 32, 46 84, 60 77, 80 21, 97
   101, 98 101, 99 101, 135 51, 136 84, 137 62, 141 24,
   145 62, 152 109, 166 26, 167 24, 168 22, 169 25, 170 54
Literature: KroegerWBHT 22

57. CONCORD

Location: New-England Psalm-Singer, p.5
         Complete Works: I, p.58
Source of text: Textless   Meter: CM
Tune type: Plain   No. of measures: 14 Key: a
   Time Sig.: 3/2 Incipit: 1543232171232
Reprints by Billings: None   Reprints by others: None
Notes: Variant versions, called ST. VINCENT'S, found in
   136 98, and 55 54. 136 variant is found in Complete
   Works, III, p.298

58. CONNECTION

Location: Singing Master's Assistant, p.99
         Complete Works: II, p.256 IV, p.296
Source of text: SMA: Watts, Psalm 48; CH: Billings?
   Meter: SM   First line: SMA: Great is the Lord our God;
   CH: Hail, sacred music, hail
Tune type: Plain No. of measures: 13 Key: E
   Time Sig.: 3/4 Incipit: 1556711765654
Reprints by Billings: 111 24; 31(frontispiece)
   Reprints by others: 22 34, 36 16, 104 14(in D), 105
   81(in D), 128 21(in D), 139 47(in D)
Notes: in 31 the tune is engraved in a circle with the

note: "This tune is thus disposed to shew that every
tune is a Compleat circle; and that what may be
deficient in the first barr, is supplied in the last."
Literature: KroegerWBHT 21(f); NathanWB 42(f)
Recordings: R

59. CONQUEST

Location: Suffolk Harmony, p.44
          Complete Works: III, p.198
Source of text: James Relly, Christian Hymns, Hymn 94
    Meter: PM [8787.12.7]   First line: Sing the triumphs of
    your conqu'ring head
Tune type: Twx verse and chorus   No. of measures: 13
    Key: C   Time Sig.: 2/2   Incipit: 5511567515123
Reprints by Billings: None   Reprints by others: 20 32, 48
    122, 49 92, 52 77, 53 77, 64 64, 151 164, 152 164, 153
    164
Literature: BarbourCM 45; Marrocco 119

60. CONSOLATION

Location: Singing Master's Assistant, p.19
          Complete Works: II, p.98
Source of text: Bedford, Specimen of Hymns, Hymn 9
    Meter: CM   First line: He's come, let ev'ry knee be
    bent
Tune type: Twx   No. of measures: 10   Key: E-flat
    Time Sig.: 6/8   Incipit: 5543432134551
Reprints by Billings: None   Reprints by others: None
Notes: BRADFORD in Waterhouse Ms 15 is a variant version.
    Reprinted in Rippon Col 66 (var, called STILLMAN)
Literature: KroegerWBM 341

61. CORSICA

Location: New-England Psalm-Singer, p.46
          Complete Works: I, p.174
Source of text: Perez Morton   Meter: CM
    First line: The Lord almighty is a God
Tune type: Twx   No. of measures: 17   Key: F

Time Sig.: 3/2   Incipit: 1345654345655
Reprints by Billings: None   Reprints by others: None
Literature: Schrader 426
Recordings: AU

62. CREATION

Location: Music in Miniature, p.3
         Complete Works: II, p.276
Source of text: Textless   Meter: CM
Tune type: Plain   No. of measures: 14 Key: G
   Time Sig.: 3/2   Incipit: 1323215436543
Reprints by Billings: 31 52 (as a fuging chorus)
   Reprints by others: None
Literature: NathanWB 31(f)

63. CREATION

Location: Continental Harmony, p.52
         Complete Works: IV, p.67
Source of text: Watts, Psalm 139, Pt.2; Watts, Hymns II,
   No.19, v.3 Meter: CM   First line: When I with
   pleasing wonder stand; Fuge: Our life contains a
   thousand springs
Tune type: Fuging chorus   No. of measures: 61 Key: F
   Time Sig.: 3/2; 3/4; 3/2; 2/2   Incipit: 1323215436543
Reprints by Billings: None   Reprints by others: None
Notes: First 15 measures published in 111 3.
Literature: BarbourCM 60,82; McKay 179(f); Mellers 14
Recordings: R, AO

64. CROSS-STREET

Location: Continental Harmony, p.56
         Complete Works: IV, p.74
Source of text: Addison, Psalm 23   Meter: PM [888888]
   First line: The Lord my pasture shall prepare
Tune type: Antiphonal verse and chorus
   No. of measures: 29 Key: C Time Sig.: 3/4; 2/4
   Incipit: 51765121S:51234
Reprints by Billings: None   Reprints by others: None

65. CRUCIFICTION

Location: Music in Miniature, p.7
         Complete Works: II, p.298
Source of text: Textless   Meter: LM
Tune type: Plain   No. of measures: 17 Key: f-sharp
   Time Sig.: 3/2 Incipit: 1543456775434
Reprints by Billings: Ind pub 5(as fuging chorus)
   Reprints by others: 70 25, 72 1, 122 1

66. CRUCIFICTION

Location: Independent publication(1787), p.5
         Complete Works: III, p.228
Source of text: Anon. in Law's Collection of Hymns,
   Hymn 34 Meter: LM First line: Mourn, mourn, ye
   saints, as if you see
Tune type: Fuging chorus   No. of measures: 38 Key: f
   Time Sig.: 3/2; 2/2 Incipit: 1543456775434
Reprints by Billings: None   Reprints by others: None
Notes: First 17 measures published in 111 7. The tunename
   followed by the note: "for good Friday."

67. CUMBERLAND

Location: New-England Psalm-Singer, p.16
         Complete Works: I, p.94
Source of text: Textless   Meter: CM
Tune type: Plain   No. of measures: 15 Key: C
   Time Sig.: 3/2 Incipit: 1342312551543
Reprints by Billings: None   Reprints by others: None

68. DANBURY

Location: Music in Miniature, p.27
         Complete Works: II, p.310
Source of text: Textless   Meter: SM
Tune type: Plain   No. of measures: 13 Key: c
   Time Sig.: 3/2 Incipit: 5123217123217
Reprints by Billings: None   Reprints by others: 68

(called CASTLET), **70** 19, **72** 3, **122** 3

69. DARTMOUTH

  Location: Waterhouse Ms, p.17
           Complete Works: II, p.264 (as NEW NORTH)
  Source of text: Watts, Hymns I, No.7 Meter: CM
    First line: Let ev'ry mortal ear attend
  Tune type: Fuging chorus   No. of measures: 30
    Key: E-flat Time Sig.: 3/2; 2/2; 3/2
    Incipit: 5543451765117
  Reprints by Billings: None   Reprints by others: None
  Manuscripts: MiU-C Ms2 119 as NEW NORTH
  Notes: Variant version of NEW NORTH published in **112** 69,
    146 67, **111** 15

70. DEDHAM

  Location: New-England Psalm-Singer, p.45
           Complete Works: I, p.170
  Source of text: Textless   Meter: LM
  Tune type: Plain   No. of measures: 16 Key: G
    Time Sig.: 3/2 Incipit: 1712323432171
  Reprints by Billings: None   Reprints by others: None
  Notes: Tunename spelled DEADHAM

71. DEDHAM

  Location: Continental Harmony, p.95
           Complete Works: IV, p.141
  Source of text: Watts, Psalm 24, v.5   Meter: LM
    First line: Rejoice, ye shining worlds on high
  Tune type: Fuging chorus   No. of measures: 35 Key: C
    Time Sig.: 2/2 Incipit: 5121234543213
  Reprints by Billings: None   Reprints by others: None
  Notes: ESSEX (**112** 65) is possibly an earlier version.
  Recordings: N

72. DELAWARE

  Location: Music in Miniature, p.28

                Complete Works: II, p.314
Source of text: Textless   Meter: LM
Tune type: Plain   No. of measures: 17 Key: c
   Time Sig.: C Incipit: 1715117117123
Reprints by Billings: None   Reprints by others: **70** 28, **72**
   4, **122** 4

73. DICKINSON

Location: New-England Psalm-Singer, p.73
              Complete Works: I, p.262
Source of text: Textless   Meter: SM
Tune type: Plain   No. of measures: 17 Key: D
   Time Sig.: C Incipit: 5134322312715
Reprints by Billings: None   Reprints by others: None

74. DIGHTON

Location: New-England Psalm-Singer, p.70
              Complete Works: I, p.250
Source of text: Textless   Meter: CM
Tune type: Plain   No. of measures: 14 Key: a
   Time Sig.: 3/2 Incipit: 1543654321551
Reprints by Billings: None   Reprints by others: None

75. DORCHESTER

Location: New-England Psalm-Singer, p.78
             Complete Works: I, p.284; II, p.60
Source of text: NEPS: Textless; SMA: Watts, Hymns II,
   No.58 Meter: CM First line: SMA: Time, what an empty
   vapour 'tis
Tune type: Plain   No. of measures: NEPS: 13 (16);
   SMA: 17 Key: f-sharp Time Sig.: NEPS:3/2; SMA:3/2;
   2/2 Incipit: 1545676543456
Reprints by Billings: **146** 9(v)   Reprints by others: **36**
   171, **141** 117
Literature: BarbourCM 51

76. DUBLIN

Location: Music in Miniature, p.26
          Complete Works: II, p.306
Source of text: Textless   Meter: SM
Tune type: Plain   No. of measures: 9 Key: f
   Time Sig.: 2/2 Incipit: 1551717656765
Reprints by Billings: None   Reprints by others: None

77. DUDLEY

Location: Music in Miniature, p.6
          Complete Works: II, p.294
Source of text: Textless   Meter: LM
Tune type: Plain   No. of measures: 16 Key: c
   Time Sig.: 3/2 Incipit: 1123212321713
Reprints by Billings: None   Reprints by others: None

78. DUNSTABLE

Location: Massachusetts Historical Society Ms.
          Complete Works: III, p.317
Source of text: Anon. Unlocated   Meter: CM
   First line: Methinks I see my saviour dear
Tune type: Plain   No. of measures: 16 Key: g
   Time Sig.: 2/2 Incipit: 1543232171232
Reprints by Billings: None   Reprints by others: None
Notes: a variant version of SAYBROOK (111 30)

79. DUNSTABLE

Location: Singing Master's Assistant, p.100
          Complete Works: II, p.258
Source of text: Watts, Psalm 42   Meter: CM
   First line: With earnest longings of the mind
Tune type: Fuging chorus   No. of measures: 49
   Key: f-sharp   Time Sig.: 3/2; 2/4
   Incipit: 1543457654345
Reprints by Billings: 111 23(first 15 measures as Plain
   tune) Reprints by others: 22 34(111 ver), 52 27(111
   ver), 53 27, 55 7(111 ver as LESSON V)

Literature: KroegerST 23, KroegerWP 51, MacDougall 53

80. DUXBOROUGH

Location: New-England Psalm-Singer, p.8
          Complete Works: I, p.70; II, p.42
Source of text: NEPS: Textless; SMA: Watts, Hymns I, No.
   24 Meter: LM First line: SMA: In vain the wealthy
   mortals toil
Tune type: Plain   No. of measures: 17 Key: e
   Time Sig.: C Incipit: 5517554551715
Reprints by Billings: **146** 3(v), **111** 9(v)
   Reprints by others: None
Manuscripts: NN Ms
Notes: Variant version called NEW HAVEN found in
   Waterhouse Ms 14 and MiU-C Ms2 124.
Literature: KroegerWBM 337

81. EAST SUDBURY

Location: Continental Harmony, p.152
          Complete Works: IV, p.226
Source of text: Watts, Psalm 148   Meter: HM
   First line: Ye tribes of Adam join
Tune type: Twx   No. of measures: 17 Key: G
   Time Sig.: 2/2 Incipit: 5313513255455
Reprints by Billings: None   Reprints by others: None

82. EAST-TOWN

Location: New-England Psalm-Singer, p.63
          Complete Works: I, p.226
Source of text: Textless   Meter: SM
Tune type: Plain   No. of measures: 13 Key: G
   Time Sig.: 3/2   Incipit: 1345434321534
Reprints by Billings: None   Reprints by others: None
Literature: BarbourCM 122

83. EASTHAM

Location: New-England Psalm-Singer, p.62

Complete Works: I, p.220
Source of text: Textless   Meter: CM
Tune type: Plain   No. of measures: 14 Key: a
    Time Sig.: 3/2 Incipit: 1345654543254
Reprints by Billings: None   Reprints by others: None

84. EDEN

Location: Suffolk Harmony, p.56
        Complete Works: III, p.220
Source of text: Watts, Hymns I, No.41   Meter: CM
    First line: Those glorious minds, how bright they shine
Tune type: Plain   No. of measures: 11. Key: F
    Time Sig.: 6/4 Incipit: 1355543466654
Reprints by Billings: None   Reprints by others: None

85. EGYPT

Location: Continental Harmony, p.61
        Complete Works: IV, p.83
Source of text: Watts, Psalm 66, v.3   Meter: CM
    First line: Come see the wonders of our God
Tune type: Fuging tune   No. of measures: 32 Key: C
    Time Sig.: 2/2 Incipit: 1171327243154
Reprints by Billings: None   Reprints by others: None

86. ELECTION

Location: Suffolk Harmony, p.40
        Complete Works: III, p.192
Source of text: John Relly, Christian Hymns, Hymn 29
    Meter: PM [11.6.6.11.11] First line: Thou art my
    blest portion, thou dear Nazarene
Tune type: Plain   No. of measures: 8 Key: g
    Time Sig.: 6/4 Incipit: 1355654555554
Reprints by Billings: None Reprints by others: 25 14,

87. EMANUEL

Location: Psalm-Singer's Amusement, p.46
        Complete Works: III, p.59

Source of text: Billings?   Meter: PM [11.11.11.11.11.11]
   First line: As shepherds in Jewry were guarding their
   sheep
Tune type: Twx verse and chorus   No. of measures: 16
   Key: G   Time Sig.: 4/4; 6/4   Incipit: 51312423531S:51
Reprints by Billings: None   Reprints by others: **54** 98(v),
   67 139(called JEWISH SHEPHERDS), **75** 56(v), **131** 121(v),
   132 85, **145** 136
Notes: Following title: "for Christmas." May be a
   recomposition of JUDEA (**146** 6). Six verses of text
   included in **120.**
Literature: BarbourCM 48; McKay 119
Recordings: B

88. EMMAUS

Location: Singing Master's Assistant, p.20
          Complete Works: II, p.102
Source of text: Perez Morton   Meter: LM
   First line: When Jesus wept a falling tear
Tune type: Plain   No. of measures: 17 Key: g
   Time Sig.: 3/2; 2/2; 3/2 Incipit: 1123531713221
Reprints by Billings: **111** 19(v) Reprints by others: **10**
   32, **22** 104, **24** 166, **36** 167, **48** 129, **49** 59, **50** 121, **63**
   99(v), **73** 49, **74** 71, **88** 129(v), **103** 19, **104** 103, **105**
   30, **143** 60, **158** 256,
Manuscripts: MHi Ms called CALVERY
Notes: Same text use in A CANON OF 4 IN 1 (**112** 56)

89. ESSEX

Location: New-England Psalm-Singer, p.65
          Complete Works: I, p.232
Source of text: Textless   Meter: SM
Tune type: Plain   No. of measures: 13 Key: C
   Time Sig.: 3/2 Incipit: 5123432123215
Reprints by Billings: None   Reprints by others: None

90. EUROPE

Location: New-England Psalm-Singer, p.90
          Complete Works: I, p.317; II, p.284
Source of text: Billings?   Meter: CM   First line: Let
   whig and torie all subside
Tune type: Fuging chorus   No. of measures: 44 (34)
   Key: F   Time Sig.: NEPS: 2/2; 3/2; MIM: 3/2
   Incipit: 1515176545554
Reprints by Billings: 111 5(rev, first 15 m. only as Plain
   tune)   Reprints by others: 70 20(111 ver), 72 4(111
   ver), 122 4(111 ver)
Manuscripts: Waterhouse Ms 3
Literature: BarbourBB 39; BarbourCM 20

91. EXETER

Location: Singing Master's Assistant, p.41
          Complete Works: II, p.152
Source of text: Watts, Hymns II, No.2   Meter: CM
   First line: My thoughts on awful subjects roll
Tune type: Twx   No. of measures: 19 Key: f
   Time Sig.: 2/2 Incipit: 1556544765434
Reprints by Billings: None   Reprints by others: 38 88, 39
   89, 88 83, 89 68(v), 117 20, 141 120

92. FAIRFIELD

Location: New-England Psalm-Singer, p.13
          Complete Works: I, p.86
Source of text: Textless   Meter: SM
Tune type: Plain   No. of measures: 13   Key: a
   Time Sig.: 3/2 Incipit: 1323454253431
Reprints by Billings: None   Reprints by others: None

93. FITCHBURGH

Location: Music in Miniature, p.3
          Complete Works: II, p.274
Source of text: Textless   Meter: LM
Tune type: Plain   No. of measures: 16 Key: a

Time Sig.: 2/2   Incipit: 1123232171132
Reprints by Billings: None   Reprints by others: **70** 26, **72**
2, **122** 2
Literature: NathanWB 31(f)

94. FRAMINGHAM

Location: Music in Miniature, p.3
         Complete Works: II, p.272
Source of text: MIM: Textless   Meter: SM
Tune type: Plain   No. of measures: 13 Key: a
   Time Sig.: 3/2 Incipit: 5121234345534
Reprints by Billings: **121** 4 (as fuging chorus)
   Reprints by others: **26** 14, **27** 14, **28** 14, **81** 16, **136** 93,
   145 195, **166** 50, **167** 50

95. FRAMINGHAM

Location: Psalm-Singer's Amusement, p.4
         Complete Works: III, p.9
Source of text: Watts, Hymns I, No.92 Meter: SM
   First line: Shall wisdom cry aloud
Tune type: Fuging chorus No. of measures: 30 Key: a
   Time Sig.: 3/2; 2/2 Incipit: 5121234345534
Reprints by Billings: **111** 3 (as Plain tune)
   Reprints by others: **26** 14, **27** 14, **28** 14, **81** 16, **136** 93,
   145 195, **166** 50, **167** 50
Literature: BarbourCM 79; NathanWB 31(f)

96. FRANKLIN

Location: Music in Miniature, p.6
         Complete Works: II, p.292
Source of text: Textless   Meter: LM
Tune type: Plain No. of measures: 16 Key: F
   Time Sig.: 3/2 Incipit: 1567176567116
Reprints by Billings: None   Reprints by others: None

97. FREEDOM

Location: New-England Psalm-Singer, p.58
          Complete Works: I, p.206
Source of text: Textless   Meter: SM
Tune type: Plain   No. of measures: 13 Key: a
    Time Sig.: 3/2 Incipit: 1323543223234
Reprints by Billings: None   Reprints by others: None
Manuscripts: CtY Ms

98. FRIENDSHIP

Location: New-England Psalm-Singer, p.61
          Complete Works: I, p.217
Source of text: Textless   Meter: SM
Tune type: Plain   No. of measures: 14 Key: A
    Time Sig.: C Incipit: 1321322234211
Reprints by Billings: None   Reprints by others: None
Notes: BENNINGTON in Waterhouse Ms 12 and MiU-C Ms2 114 is
    a variant
Literature: KroegerWBM 339

99. GEORGIA

Location: New-England Psalm-Singer, p.76
          Complete Works: I, p.274
Source of text: Textless   Meter: LM
Tune type: Plain   No. of measures: 16 Key: G
    Time Sig.: 3/2 Incipit: 1321235434325
Reprints by Billings: None   Reprints by others: None

100. GEORGIA

Location: Music in Miniature, p.31
          Complete Works: II, p.330
Source of text: Textless   Meter: LM
Tune type: Plain   No. of measures: 16 Key: g
    Time Sig.: 3/2 Incipit: 1345176543235
Reprints by Billings: None   Reprints by others: None

101. GERMANTOWN

Location: Massachusetts Historical Society Ms.
          Complete Works: III, p.318
Source of text: Watts, Hymns II, No.3   Meter: CM
   First line: Why do we mourn departing friends
Tune type: Antiphonal verse and chorus
   No. of measures: 22 Key: g   Time Sig.: 3/2; 3/4
   Incipit: S:132154T:5432155
Reprints by Billings: None   Reprints by others: None
Manuscripts: Waterhouse Ms 13(T & B only), MiU-C Ms2 109(T
   & B only), MHi Ms (4 parts)

102. GILEAD

Location: Continental Harmony, p.82
          Complete Works: IV, p.122
Source of text: Watts, Hymns II, No.88   Meter: CM
   First line: Salvation, Oh the joyful sound
Tune type: Fuging tune   No. of measures: 17 Key: C
   Time Sig.: 2/2 Incipit: 5111234445432
Reprints by Billings: None   Reprints by others: None

103. GLOCESTER

Location: Suffolk Harmony, p.47
          Complete Works: III, p.206
Source of text: James Relly, Christian Hymns, Hymn 68
   Meter: PM [66455.10] First line: Jesus, thy name we
   praise
Tune type: Plain   No. of measures: 14 Key: C
   Time Sig.: 2/2; 6/4 Incipit: 1551232116512
Reprints by Billings: None   Reprints by others: None

104. GOLGOTHA

Location: Psalm-Singer's Amusement, p.61
          Complete Works: III, p.80
Source of text: Watts, Hymns II, No.63   Meter: CM
   First line: Hark, from the tombs a doleful sound
Tune type: Twx   No. of measures: 24 Key: f

Time Sig.: 2/2   Incipit: 5171534555451
Reprints by Billings: None   Reprints by others: **17** 63, **18**
    20, **19** 20, **22** 43, **36** 170, **123** 25, **127** 30(v), **128** 30(v),
    132 122, **135** 77(v), **139** 65, **151** 165, **152** 165, **153** 165,
    154 166

105. GOSPEL POOL

Location: Ingalls, Christian Harmony, p.121
        Complete Works: II, p.237
Source of text: Newton, Olney Hymns I, No.112
    Meter: SM First line: Beside the gospel pool
Tune type: Twx   No. of measures: 9 Key: a
    Time Sig.: 2/2 Incipit: 1123454354322
Reprints by Billings: None   Reprints by others: None
Notes: Variant of mm.100-108 of Billings's anthem,
    RETROSPECT (**146** 81). It is unknown whether Billings
    himself excerpted this tune from his anthem, or whether
    it existed as a psalm-tune prior to its use in the
    anthem.

106. GREAT-PLAIN

Location: Continental Harmony, p.47
        Complete Works: IV, p.55
Source of text: Watts, Horae Lyricae, "Come Lord Jesus,"
    v.10   Meter: LM First line: Ye slumb'ring saints, a
    heav'nly host
Tune type: Fuging chorus No. of measures: 32 (33) Key: a
    Time Sig.: 3/2 Incipit: 5123217123543
Reprints by Billings: None   Reprints by others: None
Notes: At foot of CH, p.48: "Part of this tune is very
    badly bar'd, but I will leave it for the observation of
    the reader."
Literature: BarbourCM 64

107. GREENLAND

Location: New-England Psalm-Singer, p.21
        Complete Works: I, p.116
Source of text: Textless   Meter: SM

Tune type: Plain   No. of measures: 13 Key: a
   Time Sig.: 3/2 Incipit: 1342155765654
Reprints by Billings: None   Reprints by others: None

108. HACKER'S HALL

Location: Waterhouse Ms, p.9
         Complete Works: III, p.320
Source of text: Sternhold & Hopkins, Psalm 47
   Meter: CM First line: Ye people all, with one accord
Tune type: Antiphonal verse and chorus
   No. of measures: 23 Key: F Time Sig.: 2/2
   Incipit: 1215654321B:117
Reprints by Billings: None   Reprints by others: None
Manuscripts: MiU-C Ms2 108
Notes: Set for T & B only in both sources

109. HADLEY

Location: Trinity College, Hartford, Ms.
         Complete Works: III, p.322
Source of text: Anon. Meter: LM   First line: Hark,
   Hark, hear you not a cheerful noise
Tune type: Fuging tune No. of measures: 26 (31) Key: C
Time Sig.: 2/2; 3/4; 2/4   Incipit: 1111132555543
Reprints by Billings: 31 117(rev) as opening section of AN
   ANTHEM FOR CHRISTMAS Reprints by others: None
Manuscripts: MiU-C Ms3 (called HADLY)
Notes: the text appears in WilkinsBP [ca. 1750] but
   Billings's source is unknown.
Literature: KroegerWBM 325

110. HALIFAX

Location: Singing Master's Assistant, p.23
         Complete Works: II, p.111; III, p.325
Source of text: Watts, Psalm 115   Meter: PM
   [10.10.10.10.10.10] First line: Not to our names, thou
   only just and true
Tune type: Plain No. of measures: 27 Key: c
   Time Sig.: 2/2 Incipit: 5113213212231

Reprints by Billings: **111** 17   Reprints by others: None
Manuscripts: MiU-C Ms1 (v)
Literature: KroegerWBM 335

111. HAMPSHIRE

Location: New-England Psalm-Singer, p.3
          Complete Works: I, p.46
Source of text: Textless   Meter: LM
Tune type: Plain   No. of measures: 17   Key: a
   Time Sig.: C   Incipit: 1323453222343
Reprints by Billings: None   Reprints by others: None

112. HAMPSHIRE

Location: Music in Miniature, p.28
          Complete Works: II, p.312
Source of text: Textless   Meter: CM
Tune type: Plain   No. of measures: 14   Key: e
   Time Sig.: 3/2   Incipit: 5517534555343
Reprints by Billings: None   Reprints by others: **70** 30, **71**
   5, **72** 6, **122** 5

113. HAMTON

Location: New-England Psalm-Singer, p.14
          Complete Works: I, p.90
Source of text: Textless   Meter: LM
Tune type: Plain   No. of measures: 16   Key: C
   Time Sig.: 3/2   Incipit: 1121765671711
Reprints by Billings: None   Reprints by others: None

114. HANOVER

Location: New-England Psalm-Singer, p.75
          Complete Works: I, p.271
Source of text: Billings?   Meter: LM
   First line: Bless'd is the man, supremely bless'd
Tune type: Plain   No. of measures: 17   Key: D
   Time Sig.: C   Incipit: 1516517116561
Reprints by Billings: None   Reprints by others: None

Literature: BarbourCM 122

115. HANOVER NEW

Location: New-England Psalm-Singer, p.75
          Complete Works: I, p.272
Source of text: Textless   Meter: CM
Tune type: Plain   No. of measures: 14   Key: A
   Time Sig.: 3/2   Incipit: 1356543255432
Reprints by Billings: None   Reprints by others: None

116. HARTFORD

Location: Psalm-Singer's Amusement, p.103
          Complete Works: III, p.168
Source of text: James Relly, Christian Hymns, No.84
   Meter: PM [85857785]   First line: Glorious Jesus,
   glorious Jesus, thy dear name to praise
Tune type: Antiphonal Twx   No. of measures: 30   Key: G
   Time Sig.: 2/4   Incipit: 1513272432345
Reprints by Billings: **144** 25(v)   Reprints by others: **64**
   55, **81** 12, **136** 15, **166** 20
Notes: Varied reprint in WilliamsPE, v.2, p.131, called
   NEW ENGLAND.

117. HARVARD

Location: New-England Psalm-Singer, p.68
          Complete Works: I, p.245
Source of text: Textless   Meter: CM
Tune type: Plain   No. of measures: 15   Key: d
   Time Sig.: C   Incipit: 1517757112343
Reprints by Billings: None   Reprints by others: None

118. HATFIELD

Location: Shumway, American Harmony, p.137
          Complete Works: III, p.282; III, p.284
Source of text: Watts, Hymns I, No.5   Meter: CM
   First line: Naked as from the earth we came
Tune type: Twx   No. of measures: 16   Key: g

Time Sig.: 2/2   Incipit: 1123453112343
Reprints by Billings: None   Reprints by others: **70** 29(v),
72 5(v), **75** 34(var, called THE TRUE PENITENT), **122** 5(v)
Manuscripts: CtY Ms (v)
Literature: BarbourCM 86

119. HATFIELD

Location: Waterhouse Ms, p.1
          Complete Works: III, p.328
Source of text: John Peck, "A Poem on Death," in
    Description, v.6 Meter: CM First line: Though beauty
    grace the comely face
Tune type: Plain   No. of measures: 11 Key: a
    Time Sig.: 2/2 Incipit: 1323542751543
Reprints by Billings: None   Reprints by others: None
Notes: Incomplete: only first half of Treble, and no
    Counter; Ms dated 30 May 1780.

120. HAVERILL

Location: New-England Psalm-Singer, p.96
          Complete Works: I, p.335
Source of text: Brady & Tate, Psalm 34   Meter: CM
    First line: Through all the changing scenes of life
Tune type: Antiphonal verse and chorus
    No. of measures: 22 (23) Key: G Time Sig.: 3/2
    Incipit: B:11765154321T:34
Reprints by Billings: None   Reprints by others: None

121. HEATH

Location: Singing Master's Assistant, p.11
          Complete Works: II, p.69
Source of text: T. Flatman, Poems, "Hymne for the Morning"
    Meter: LM First line: Awake my soul, awake my eyes
Tune type: Fuging tune   No. of measures: 29 Key: C
    Time Sig.: 2/2 Incipit: 5111133335531
Reprints by Billings: None   Reprints by others: None

122. HEBRON

Location: New-England Psalm-Singer, p.69
          Complete Works: I, p.246; II, p.86
Source of text: NEPS: Textless; SMA: Watts, Hymns II,
    No.93 Meter: SM First line: My God, my life, my love
Tune type: Plain   No. of measures: 13 Key: d
   Time Sig.: 3/2 Incipit: 5171232321132
Reprints by Billings: 146 15(v), 111 14(v)
    Reprints by others: 80 12(v), 136 67(v), 153 129, 154
    129(v), 155 83, 166 65(v)
Manuscripts: MB Ms

123. HEBRON

Location: Pilsbury, United States Sacred Harmony, p.145
          Complete Works: III, p.286
Source of text: Anon. in KnappNCM, 2d ed., p.162
    Meter: PM [886886] First line: Behold the splendor,
    hear the shout
Tune type: Antiphonal Fuging tune   No. of measures: 28
    Key: E   Time Sig.: 2/2 Incipit: 5117517111121
Reprints by Billings: None   Reprints by others: 103 108
Notes: Variant version of NORTHBOROUGH (144 17)
Literature: BarbourCM 85,115

124. HINGHAM

Location: New-England Psalm-Singer, p.7
          Complete Works: I, p.62
Source of text: Textless   Meter: SM
Tune type: Plain   No. of measures: 14 Key: b
   Time Sig.: C Incipit: 1712322312713
Reprints by Billings: None   Reprints by others: 52 57,
    119 89
Notes: See NEW HINGHAM (112 59) for variant version

125. HOLDEN

Location: New-England Psalm-Singer, p.88

Complete Works: I, p.312
Source of text: Textless   Meter: PM [888888]
Tune type: Plain   No. of measures: 24 Key: C
   Time Sig.: 3/2   Incipit: 1132143223143
Reprints by Billings: None   Reprints by others: None

126. HOLLIS

Location: New-England Psalm-Singer, p.86
            Complete Works: I, p.306
Source of text: Textless   Meter: LM
Tune type: Plain No. of measures: 16 Key: B-flat
   Time Sig.: 3/2   Incipit: 1543671567116
Reprints by Billings: None   Reprints by others: None

127. HOLLIS STREET

Location: New-England Psalm-Singer, p.94
            Complete Works: I, p.329; II, p.88
Source of text: NEPS: Mather Byles; SMA: Charles Wesley,
   from Whitefield Collection, Hymn 50   Meter: PM
   [55556565] First line: NEPS: Let angels above and
   saints here below; SMA: Ye servants of God, your
   master proclaim
Tune type: Plain   No. of measures: 16 Key: F
   Time Sig.: 3/2   Incipit: 1356176545567
Reprints by Billings: 146 16(v) Reprints by others: None
Notes: in 146 Billings credits the text to G. Whitefield.

128. HOPKINTON

Location: Continental Harmony, p.144
            Complete Works: IV, p.214
Source of text: John Cennick, in Whitefield Collection,
   Hymn 55 (p.164) Meter: PM [8787.12.7]   First line:
   Lo, he cometh, countless trumpets
Tune type: Antiphonal Fuging Tune   No. of measures: 29
   Key: B-flat Time Sig.: 2/4 Incipit: 1513312727242
Reprints by Billings: None   Reprints by others: None
Recordings: R

129. HULL

  Location: Suffolk Harmony, p.46
            Complete Works: III, p.204
  Source of text: James Relly, Christian Hymns, Hymn 58
    Meter: PM [886886] First line: We celebrate the praise
    to day
  Tune type: Twx   No. of measures: 14 Key: G
    Time Sig.: 2/2 Incipit: 1334554332132
  Reprints by Billings: None   Reprints by others: 22 53

130. HYMN FOR CHRISTMAS, AN

  Location: New-England Psalm-Singer, p.15
            Complete Works: I, p.92
  Source of text: Brady & Tate, Supplement, Hymn 11
    Meter: CM First line: While shepherds watch'd their
    flocks by night
  Tune type: Twx   No. of measures: 17 Key: F
    Time Sig.: 2/2 Incipit: 1334321556543
  Reprints by Billings: None   Reprints by others: None
  Notes: alternate tunename: CHARLSTON; in 112 Billings
    cites as the text source "Hymn 26" (i.e., Hymn 26 in
    Appendix).
  Recordings: B

131. INVOCATION

  Location: Continental Harmony, p.57
            Complete Works: IV, p.76
  Source of text: Billings?   Meter: LM
    First line: Majestic God, our muse inspire
  Tune type: Fuging chorus   No. of measures: 28 Key: C
    Time Sig.: 2/2; 6/4 Incipit: 5111231765A:534
  Reprints by Billings: None   Reprints by others: None
  Notes: Text appears on title page of 146

132. IPSWICH

  Location: New-England Psalm-Singer, p.72
            Complete Works: I, p.258

Source of text: Textless   Meter: CM
Tune type: Plain   No. of measures: 15 Key: a
    Time Sig.: C Incipit: 1232542122321
Reprints by Billings: None   Reprints by others: None

133. JAMAICA

Location: New-England Psalm-Singer, p.64
          Complete Works: I, p.230
Source of text: Textless   Meter: LM
Tune type: Plain   No. of measures: 16 Key: a
    Time Sig.: 3/2 Incipit: 1751275314257
Reprints by Billings: None   Reprints by others: None
Notes: title spelled JAMACIA

134. JAMAICA

Location: Music in Miniature, p.4
          Complete Works: II, p.282
Source of text: Textless   Meter: CM
Tune type: Plain   No. of measures: 14 Key: F
    Time Sig.: 3/2 Incipit: 5671565553517
Reprints by Billings: None   Reprints by others: **70** 23, **72**
    7, **122** 7

135. JARGON

Location: Singing-Master's Assistant, p.102
          Complete Works: II, p.263
Source of text: Billings   Meter: PM [8787]
    First line: Let horrid jargon split the air
Tune type: Plain   No. of measures: 14 Key: G
    Time Sig.: 2/2 Incipit: 1643651665131
Reprints by Billings: None   Reprints by others: **141** 131
Notes: the text is also used at the end of the anthem: By
    the Rivers of Watertown (LAMENTATION OVER BOSTON).
Literature: BarbourCM 99; Gryc 22; MacDougall 55; Marrocco
    113
Recordings: R

136. JERUSALEM

Location: Suffolk Harmony, p.42
           Complete Works: III, p.196
Source of text: James Relly, Christian Hymns, Hymn 40
   Meter: PM [77775777] First line: All is hush, the
   battle's o'er
Tune type: Plain   No. of measures: 31 Key: E-flat
   Time Sig.: 2/4 Incipit: 1717654365671
Reprints by Billings: None   Reprints by others: None

137. JORDAN

Location: Suffolk Harmony, p.33
           Complete Works: III, p.180
Source of text: Watts, Hymns II, No.66, v.1,3
   Meter: CM First line: There is a land of pure delight
Tune type: Antiphonal Twx   No. of measures: 32 Key: A
   Time Sig.: 2/2 Incipit: 5113212323432
Reprints by Billings: None   Reprints by others: **8** 26(v),
   11 20, **12** 20, **13** 20, **19** 143, **20** 48, **22** 68, **23** 72(v), **24**
   72, **32** 58, **33** 58, **36** 70, **40** no.65(v), **41** 77, **42** 38, **43**
   38, **44** 45, **45** 13(v), **46** 106, **50** 41, **51** 100, **56** 81(v),
   61 29, **62** 195, **63** 126, **64** 52, **65** 52, **66** 37, **68** 359, **69**
   45, **70** 22, **72** 6, **89** 94(v), **91** 45, **92** 46, **93** 46, **94** 46,
   95 46, **96** 25, **97** 25, **98** 25, **99** 25, **100** 25, **101** 25, **102**
   28, **103** 54, **104** 40, **105** 84, **107** 19, **108** 19, **109** 64, **110**
   21, **113** 30, **116** 62, **119** 26(v), **120** 30, **129** 34, **130** 34,
   132 119, **135** 96, **138** 23, **143** 34, **150** 48, **151** 48, **152**
   52, **153** 52, **154** 52, **155** 50, **156** 50, **157** 50, **158** 50, **159**
   50, **160** 50, **161** 50, **162** 50, **163** 50, **164** 50, **167** 112,
   168 81, **169** 70, **170** 35, **171** 35, **172** 45, **173** 81, **178**
   102, **179** 102
Literature: CrawfordCR xxxviii; CrawfordMM 597(f)
Recordings: A

138. JUDEA

Location: Singing-Master's Assistant, p.6
           Complete Works: II, p.52

Source of text: Anon. in ArnoldCP, Book IV, p.5
    Meter: PM [11.11.11.11.11.11]   First line: A virgin
    unspotted the prophet foretold
Tune type: Antiphonal verse and chorus
    No. of measures: 12   Key: F Time Sig.: 6/4; 6/8
    Incipit: 1131242312132
Reprints by Billings: None   Reprints by others: None
Notes: EMANUEL (in 121 46) may be a variant
Literature: BarbourCM 47, 114; Stevenson (f fig.8),
    KroegerWP 53
Recordings: C, K, R, S, X, AE, AO, AP

139. KITTERY

Location: Brownson, Select Harmony, p.17
            Complete Works: III, p.152; III, p.288
Source of text: Brady & Tate, Supplement, Hymn 8
    Meter: CM First line: Our Father who in heaven art
Tune type: Fuging tune No. of measures: 18 Key: a
    Time Sig.: 2/2 Incipit: 1171233221232
Reprints by Billings: 144 12   Reprints by others: 22 56,
    27 17, 28 17, 64 57, 65 55, 89 96(v), 91 35(v), 135
    101, 145 156, 150 68, 151 68, 152 68, 170 19, 171 20
Manuscripts: CtHT-W Ms (v), MHi Ms (v), MiU-C Ms1 (v)
Notes: Brownson's print, which predates Billings's by
    about 3 years, varies slightly from it in several
    places (e.g., mm.11-12, 17). Brownson's print is
    called KETTERY. Billings attributes the text to Watts
    in 144.
Recordings: R, S

140. LANCASTER

Location: New-England Psalm-Singer, p.43
            Complete Works: I, p.324
Source of text: Textless   Meter: LM
Tune type: Plain No. of measures: 17 Key: a
    Time Sig.: C Incipit: 1534534253422
Reprints by Billings: None   Reprints by others: None
Notes: SHIRLEY (112 74) is a transposed version
Literature: BarbourCM 120

141. LARK, THE

Location: Independent Publication (1790)
          Complete Works: III, p.232
Source of text: Anon., Unlocated   Meter: LM
    First line: Look up and see th'unwearied sun
Tune type: Antiphonal Twx   No. of measures: 42   Key: C
    Time Sig.: 2/4   Incipit: 5112171233334
Reprints by Billings: None   Reprints by others: 122
    (paged sep. at end)
Notes: the text appeared in WarnerSMG but Billings's
    source of the text is unknown.

142. LEBANON

Location: New-England Psalm-Singer, p.95
          Complete Works: I, p.333; II, p.78
Source of text: Billings   Meter: CM
    First line: Death with his warrant in his hand
Tune Type: Plain   No. of measures: NEPS: 8; SMA: 15
    Key: NEPS: g; SMA: a   Time Sig.: NEPS: 4/4; SMA: 2/2
    Incipit: 1321712345565
Reprints by Billings: 146 14(v), 111 9(v)
    Reprints by others: 10 51, 22 72, 35 69(v), 36 78, 52
    17, 53 17, 59 55, 60 31, 62 213, 66 55, 67 59, 76 26,
    78 37, 79 54, 89 99(v), 91 29(v), 92 30, 93 30, 94 30,
    95 30, 96 28, 97 23, 98 23, 99 23, 100 23, 101 23, 102
    26, 104 9, 136 72, 141 119, 145 141, 150 63, 151 63,
    152 63, 153 63, 154 63, 155 48, 156 48, 157 48, 158 48,
    166 63, 167 63, 168 37, 169 26, 170 39, 171 45, 172 23,
    173 23, 178 95, 179 95
Manuscripts: NN Ms 1
Literature: BarbourBB 39; BarbourCM 15; CrawfordCR x1;
    Stevenson 62

143. LEWIS-TOWN

Location: Continental Harmony, p.198
          Complete Works: IV, p.292
Source of text: Brady & Tate, Psalm 133, v.1; Watts,

Psalm 133, v.4, 3 <u>Meter</u>: CM   <u>First line</u>: B&T: How
vast must their advantage be; Watts: 'Tis pleasant at
the morning dew
<u>Tune</u> <u>type</u>: Antiphonal Twx   <u>No. of measures</u>: 27
  <u>Key:</u> C;c;C <u>Time Sig.</u>: 2/2; 6/4; 6/8
  <u>Incipit</u>: 1123143213121
<u>Reprints by Billings</u>: None   <u>Reprints by others</u>: None
<u>Notes</u>: the third strain of this tune is a rhythmic
  recasting of the first.

144. LEXINGTON

<u>Location</u>: New-England Psalm-Singer, p.66
          Complete Works: I, p.236
<u>Source of text</u>: Textless   <u>Meter</u>: LM
<u>Tune type</u>: Plain <u>No. of measures</u>: 16 <u>Key:</u> a
  <u>Time Sig.</u>: 3/4 <u>Incipit</u>: 1345432123223
<u>Reprints by Billings</u>: None   <u>Reprints by others</u>: None
<u>Notes</u>: WEYMOUTH (**31** 74) is a possible later version.

145. LIBERTY

<u>Location</u>: New-England Psalm-Singer, p.9
          Complete Works: I, p.75
<u>Source of text</u>: Billings?   <u>Meter</u>: SM
  <u>First line</u>: God bless our gracious king
<u>Tune type</u>: Plain <u>No. of measures</u>: 13 <u>Key:</u> G
  <u>Time Sig.</u>: 3/2 <u>Incipit</u>: 1356543212345
<u>Reprints by Billings</u>: None   <u>Reprints by others</u>: None
<u>Literature</u>: NathanWB 20(f)

146. LINCOLN

<u>Location</u>: New-England Psalm-Singer, p.77
          Complete Works: I, p.278
<u>Source of text</u>: Textless   <u>Meter</u>: SM
<u>Tune type</u>: Plain <u>No. of measures</u>: 13 <u>Key:</u> C
  <u>Time Sig.</u>: 3/2 <u>Incipit</u>: 1123517116513
<u>Reprints by Billings</u>: None   <u>Reprints by others</u>: None

147. LYNN

Location: New-England Psalm-Singer, p.70
          Complete Works: I, p.252
Source of text: Textless   Meter: CM
Tune type: Plain No. of measures: 14 Key: G
   Time Sig.: 3/2 Incipit: 1343215654345
Reprints by Billings: None   Reprints by others: None

148. MADRID

Location: Music in Miniature, p.32
          Complete Works: II, p.332
Source of text: MIM: Textless; SH: James Relly, Christian
   Hymns, Hymn 87   Meter: PM [55556565]
   First line: How charmingly sounds the word of the Lord
Tune type: Plain   No. of measures: 17 Key: C
   Time Sig.: 2/2 Incipit: 5117132176551
Reprints by Billings: **144** 24   Reprints by others: **10** 56,
   22 38, **28** 58, **63** 54, **70** 26, **72** 2, **89** 110(v), **122** 2, **142**
   13(v), **143** 13, **145** 151, **170** 58

149. MAJESTY

Location: Singing Master's Assistant, p.68
          Complete Works: II, p.203
Source of text: Sternhold & Hopkins, Psalm 18, v.9-10
   Meter: CM First line: The Lord descended from above
Tune type: Antiphonal Twx   No. of measures: 29 Key: F
   Time Sig.: 2/2 Incipit: 5171653143117
Reprints by Billings: None   Reprints by others: **1** 42, **2**
   42, **3** 42, **4** 62, **5** 62, **6** 62, **8** 81, **11** 46, **12** 46, **13** 46,
   17 64, **18** 23, **19** 23, **21** 22, **22** 84(v), **38** 74, **39** 74, **41**
   95, **46** 77, **50** 50, **56** 84(v), **60** 21, **61** 24, **62** 2, **63** 75,
   65 68, **66** 10, **73** 38, **74** 40, **84** 26, **89** 105, **96** 80, **97**
   80, **98** 80, **99** 80, **100** 80, **101** 80, **102** 85, **103** 58, **104**
   32, **105** 32, **109** 76, **110** 22(v), **119** 23, **124** 75, **125** 51,
   127 13, **128** 13, **129** 19, **130** 19, **131** 60, **132** 41, **135**
   113, **136** 77, **137** 49(v), **138** 27, **139** 50, **140** 3, **141** 19,
   143 33, **145** 49(v), **147** 40, **150** 22, **151** 22, **152** 34, **153**

34, **154** 34, **155** 30, **156** 30, **157** 30, **158** 30, **159** 30, **172**
10, **173** 58, **178** 117, **179** 117
Literature: BarbourCM 114; CrawfordCR xlii; MacDougall
    64(f); McKay 90
Recordings: AS

150. MALDEN

Location: New-England Psalm-Singer, p.4
        Complete Works: I, p.51
Source of text: Textless (Brady & Tate, Psalm 106)
    Meter: LM   First line: O render thanks to God above
Tune type: Plain   No. of measures: 16   Key: G
    Time Sig.: 3/2   Incipit: 1345534565432
Reprints by Billings: None   Reprints by others: None
Manuscripts: MiU-C Ms2 115(T & B only), NN Ms
Notes: Although textless, Billings suggests "Ps.106"
    (i.e., Brady & Tate, Psalm 106) as a text.

151. MANCHESTER

Location: Music in Miniature, p.5
        Complete Works: II, p.286
Source of text: Textless   Meter: LM
Tune type: Plain   No. of measures: 16   Key: E
    Time Sig.: 2/2   Incipit: 5671121765517
Reprints by Billings: **121** 6 (as Fuging chorus)
    Reprints by others: **36** 172, **104** 38, **123** 32, **135** 111,
    145 144, **167** 110, **168** 82, **169** 71, **170** 40, **171** 36, **179**
    128

152. MANCHESTER

Location: Psalm-Singer's Amusement, p.6
        Complete Works: III, p.12
Source of text: Brady & Tate, Psalm 150, v.3-4
    Meter: LM   First line: Let the shrill trumpet's warlike
    voice
Tune type: Fuging chorus   No. of measures: 43   Key: E
    Time Sig.: 2/2; 2/4   Incipit: 5671121765517
Reprints by Billings: None   Reprints by others: **36** 172,

104 38, **123** 32, **135** 111, **145** 144, **167** 110, **168** 82, **169**
71, **170** 40, **171** 36, **179** 128
Notes: printed in **111** 5 as Plain tune.

153. MANSFIELD

Location: Music in Miniature, p.30
           Complete Works: II, p.322
Source of text: Textless   Meter: PM [888888]
Tune type: Plain No. of measures: 24 Key: f-sharp
   Time Sig.: 3/2 Incipit: 1543451754355
Reprints by Billings: None Reprints by others: **70** 27, **72**
  3, **122** 3

154. MANSFIELD

Location: Worcester Collection, 2d ed., p.105
           Complete Works: III, p.290
Source of text: Watts, Psalm 148, v.11-12   Meter: LM
  First line: Jehovah, 'tis a glorious word
Tune type: Twx No. of measures: 34 Key: F
   Time Sig.: 2/2 Incipit: 1351167112176
Reprints by Billings: None Reprints by others: **22** 31,
  168 72
Notes: not attributed to Billings in **167** or **168**, but the
  printing in **22** carries his name.

155. MARBLEHEAD

Location: New-England Psalm-Singer, p.71
           Complete Works: I, p.256; II, p.80
Source of text: NEPS: Textless; SMA: Brady & Tate, Psalm
  133 Meter: CM First line: How vast must their
  advantage be
Tune type: Plain No. of measures: 14 Key: G
   Time Sig.: 3/2 Incipit: 1565434321213
Reprints by Billings: **146** 14(v) Reprints by others: None

156. MARSHFIELD

Location: New-England Psalm-Singer, p.76
          Complete Works: I, p.276; II, p.84
Source of text: NEPS: Textless; SMA: Brady & Tate, Psalm
   137 Meter: LM   First line: When we our weary'd limbs
   to rest
Tune type: Plain   No. of measures: 16 Key: e
   Time Sig.: 3/2 Incipit: 1345476513217
Reprints by Billings: 146 15(v), 111 23(v)
   Reprints by others: 22 47, 68 12(v)
Notes: Varied reprint in WilliamsPE, v.2, p.96.

157. MARYLAND

Location: Singing Master's Assistant, p.29
          Complete Works: II, p.126
Source of text: Watts, Hymns II, No.110   Meter: SM
   First line: And must this body die
Tune type: Fuging chorus No. of measures: 20 Key: a
   Time Sig.: 2/2 Incipit: 1354322354321
Reprints by Billings: 111 13(as Plain tune)
   Reprints by others: 1 22, 2 22, 3 22, 4 42, 5 42, 6
   42, 14 38, 15 38, 22 42, 38 55, 39 95, 44 19, 49 25, 61
   21, 63 97(v), 76 74, 81 26, 82 20, 84 16, 91 69, 92 70,
   93 70, 94 70, 95 70, 104 49, 119 79(v), 124 84, 125 60,
   136 90, 137 52(v), 138 28, 140 6, 141 22, 145 52(v),
   150 75(v), 151 75, 152 76(v), 153 76, 154 76(v), 166
   53, 167 20, 168 19(v), 169 19, 170 42, 171 39, 178 114,
   179 114
Literature: BarbourCM 84; CrawfordCR xliii

158. MASSACHUSETTS

Location: New-England Psalm-Singer, p.40
          Complete Works: I, p.153
Source of text: Perez Morton   Meter: PM [10.10.11.11]
   First line: Great is the Lord God, the thunder's his
   voice
Tune type: Plain No. of measures: 16 Key: C

Time Sig.: 3/2   Incipit: 5132123543211
Reprints by Billings: None   Reprints by others: None
Notes: title spelled MASSECHUSTTS.

159. MEDFIELD

Location: New-England Psalm-Singer, p.94
          Complete Works: I, p.330; II, p.66
Source of text: Samuel Byles, Pious Remains, p.6
  Meter: LM First line: When I my various blessings see
Tune type: Plain   No. of measures: 16 Key: C
   Time Sig.: 3/8   Incipit: 5125143223454
Reprints by Billings: 146 10(v) Reprints by others: 141
   118
Notes: MORRISTON in Waterhouse Ms 4 and MiU-C Ms2 112 is a
   variant
Literature: KroegerWBM 337

160. MEDFORD

Location: New-England Psalm-Singer, p.86
          Complete Works: I, p.304
Source of text: Textless   Meter: LM
Tune type: Plain No. of measures: 16 Key: b
   Time Sig.: 3/2   Incipit: 1321276513457
Reprints by Billings: None   Reprints by others: None

161. MEDWAY

Location: Singing Master's Assistant, p.18
          Complete Works: II, p.94
Source of text: Watts, Psalm 95   Meter: CM
  First line: Sing to the Lord Jehovah's name
Tune type: Fuging chorus   No. of measures: 38 Key: G
   Time Sig.: 3/4; 2/4 Incipit: 1555532155671
Reprints by Billings: None   Reprints by others: None
Literature: McKay 94(f)

162. MENDOM

Location: Psalm-Singer's Amusement, p.53
         Complete Works: III, p.170
Source of text: John Relly, Christian Hymns, Hymn 17
   Meter: PM [76767876] First line: My redeemer let me be
Tune type: Twx   No. of measures: 18 Key: a
   Time Sig.: 2/2 Incipit: 1175171235432
Reprints by Billings: **144** 27   Reprints by others: **22** 52,
   36 151, **52** 75, **53** 75, **63** 60, **81** 13, **82** 16, **83** 38, **103**
   140, **119** 140, **135** 116, **136** 92, **137** 48, **138** 22, **145** 48,
   166 57, **180** 106
Notes: In many reprints the tunename is MENDON

163. MIDDLESEX

Location: New-England Psalm-Singer, p.62
         Complete Works: I, p.222
Source of text: Textless   Meter: CM
Tune type: Antiphonal Plain   No. of measures: 13 (14)
   Key: G   Time Sig.: 3/2 Incipit: 1335143212354
Reprints by Billings: None   Reprints by others: None

164. MIDDLETOWN

Location: New-England Psalm-Singer, p.74
         Complete Works: I, p.267
Source of text: Textless   Meter: SM
Tune type: Plain   No. of measures: 16 Key: g
   Time Sig.: 2/4 Incipit: 1353213557655
Reprints by Billings: None   Reprints by others: None

165. MILTON

Location: New-England Psalm-Singer, p.44
         Complete Works: I, p.167
Source of text: Sternhold & Hopkins and Brady & Tate,
   Psalm 145   Meter: CM   First line: Thee will I laud,
   my God and king
Tune type: Fuging chorus   No. of measures: 30 Key: G
   Time Sig.: 3/2 Incipit: 1321234543432

Reprints by Billings: None   Reprints by others: None
Notes: the composite text was probably made by Billings
     himself.
Literature: BarbourCM 55

166. MORAVIA

Location: Suffolk Harmony, p.50
          Complete Works: III, p.212
Source of text: James Relly, Christian Hymns, Hymn 16
     Meter: PM [11.11.10.11.11.11]   First line: O love,
     what a secret to mortals thou art
Tune type: Antiphonal Twx   No. of measures: 13   Key: C
     Time Sig.: 6/4   Incipit: 51176712755S:23
Reprints by Billings: None   Reprints by others: None

167. MORIAH

Location: Suffolk Harmony, p.39
          Complete Works: III, p.190
Source of text: John Relly, Christian Hymns, Hymn 8
     Meter: PM [10.10.10.10]   First line: All over lovely
     is my Lord and God
Tune type: Plain   No. of measures: 16   Key: D
     Time Sig.: 2/4   Incipit: 5551156712222
Reprints by Billings: None   Reprints by others: None

168. MORNING HYMN

Location: Continental Harmony, p.68
          Complete Works: IV, p.98
Source of text: Watts, Hymns II, No.6   Meter: CM
     First line: Once more my soul the rising day
Tune type: Fuging tune   No. of measures: 22   Key: C
     Time Sig.: 2/2   Incipit: 5132171765671
Reprints by Billings: None   Reprints by others: None
Literature: BarbourCM 59

169. MORPHEUS

Location: Music in Miniature, p.8

Complete Works: II, p.302, p.337
Source of text: Textless   Meter: LM
Tune type: Plain   No. of measures: 16 Key: a
   Time Sig.: 2/2 Incipit: 5321234553451
Reprints by Billings: None   Reprints by others: **48** 128,
   49 58, **54** 58
Manuscripts: Waterhouse Ms 9(T & B only) contains a fuging
   section not included in the printed versions (see
   Complete Works: II, p.337).
Notes: Although textless and without a suggested text in
   111, all reprints and Ms copies set the Flatman poem
   "Sleep, downy sleep come close my eyes," which may have
   been Billings's intended text.
Recordings: R, AN

170. MORRISTON

Location: Waterhouse Ms, p.4
         Complete Works: III, p.330
Source of text: Watts, Hymns II, No.146   Meter: LM
   First line: Man has a soul of vast desires
Tune type: Plain   No. of measures: 17 Key: C
   Time Sig.: 2/2 Incipit: 5671251432122
Reprints by Billings: None   Reprints by others: None
Manuscripts: MiU-C Ms2 112
Notes: Ascribed to Billings on the basis of its being a
   variant of MEDFIELD. Waterhouse Ms has the initials
   "SH" following the meter designation, which may stand
   for Susanna Heath, the compiler.
Literature: KroegerWBM 337

171. NANTASKET

Location: New-England Psalm-Singer, p.41
         Complete Works: I, p.158
Source of text: Textless   Meter: LM
Tune type: Plain   No. of measures: 16 Key: C
   Time Sig.: 3/2 Incipit: 1323217123225
Reprints by Billings: None   Reprints by others: None

172. NANTUCKET

Location: New-England Psalm-Singer, p.2
          Complete Works: I, p.44
Source of text: Textless (Watts, Hymns I, No.10)
   Meter: SM First line: How beauteous are their feet
Tune type: Plain   No. of measures: 13 Key: D
   Time Sig.: 3/2 Incipit: 5143217115176
Reprints by Billings: None   Reprints by others: None
Notes: Although textless, Billings suggests "Hymn 5"
   (i.e., Hymn 5 in Appendix) as the text.

173. NAZARETH

Location: Music in Miniature, p.6
          Complete Works: II, p.290
Source of text: Textless   Meter: CM
Tune type: Plain   No. of measures: 15 Key: g
   Time Sig.: 3/2 Incipit: 1547654345432
Reprints by Billings: None   Reprints by others: None

174. NEW BOSTON

Location: New-England Psalm-Singer, p.6
          Complete Works: I, p.60
Source of text: Textless (Brady & Tate, Psalm 148)
   Meter: HM   First line: Ye boundless realms of joy
Tune type: Plain   No. of measures: 21 Key: D
   Time Sig.: C Incipit: 1321711712322
Reprints by Billings: None   Reprints by others: None
Notes: Although textless, Billings suggests "Ps.148"
   (i.e., Brady & Tate, Psalm 148) as the text.
Literature: BarbourCM 120

175. NEW-CASTLE

Location: Music in Miniature, p.4
          Complete Works: II, p.278
Source of text: Textless   Meter: CM
Tune type: Plain   No. of measures: 15 Key: D
   Time Sig.: 4/4   Incipit: 1171231222311

Reprints by Billings: None   Reprints by others: None

176. NEW HAVEN

Location: Waterhouse Ms 14   Complete Works: III, p.332
Source of text: Anon. Unlocated   Meter: LM
   First line: Come now my soul, my heart, my tongue
Tune type: Plain   No. of measures: 10   Key: f-sharp
   Time Sig.: 6/4; 3/2   Incipit: 5517553455171
Reprints by Billings: None   Reprints by others: None
Manuscripts: MiU-C Ms2 124
Notes: Ascribed to Billings on the basis of it being a
   variant of DUXBOROUGH
Literature: KroegerWBM 337

177. NEW HINGHAM

Location: New-England Psalm-Singer, p.59
         Complete Works: I, p.209; II, p.83
Source of text: Billings   Meter: SM
   First line: Death, O the awful sound
Tune type: Plain   No. of measures: NEPS: 10; SMA: 11
   Key: NEPS: b; SMA: a   Time Sig.: 2/2
   Incipit: NEPS: 1712322312713; SMA: 1712322312712
Reprints by Billings: 146 15(v), 111 16(v)
   Reprints by others: 46 87, 80 32, 89 116(called
   NEWINGHAM), 91 70, 136 87, 140 60, 141 68(called
   NEWINGHAM), 145 131, 150 72, 151 72, 166 39, 176
   27(called NEWINGHAM)
Literature: BarbourCM 123

178. NEW NORTH

Location: New-England Psalm-Singer, p.69
         Complete Works: I, p.248; II, p.200, p.264
Source of text: NEPS: Textless; SMA: Brady & Tate, Psalm
   135 Meter: CM First line: O praise the Lord with one
   consent
Tune type: Plain   No. of measures: 18   Key: D
   Time Sig.: C   Incipit: 5534516517654
Reprints by Billings: 146 67(v), 111 15(v)

Reprints by others: **80** 30
Manuscripts: Waterhouse Ms 17 called DARTMOUTH; MiU-C Ms2
    called NEW NORTH; both Ms copies include a fuging
    section not published by Billings. The text set is
    Watts, Hymns I, No.7.
Literature: BarbourCM 117

179. NEW-PLYMOUTH

Location: Continental Harmony, p.169
          Complete Works: IV, p.251
Source of text: Brady & Tate, Psalm 44, v.1-2
    Meter: CM   First line: O Lord, our fathers oft have
    told
Tune type: Fuging chorus   No. of measures: 25   Key: C
    Time Sig.: 2/2   Incipit: 1123143221171
Reprints by Billings: None   Reprints by others: None
Notes: Note at head: "Suitable to be sung on the
    Anniversary of our Forefathers' landing in New England,
    Nov. 20th. Anno Domini 1620." Note at foot: Rouse ye
    Yankees and celebrate this Anniversary, and do not say
    on the 21st. day of November, 'I forgot what day it was
    yesterday.'"
Recordings: AO

180. NEW SOUTH

Location: New-England Psalm-Singer, p.12
          Complete Works: I, p.80; II, p.64
Source of text: NEPS: Textless; SMA: Brady & Tate, Psalm
    67   Meter: SM First line: To bless thy chosen race
Tune type: Plain   No. of measures: 15   Key: C
    Time Sig.: 3/2   Incipit: 1171322312711
Reprints by Billings: **146** 10(v), **111** 9(v)
    Reprints by others: **80** 12

181. NEW TOWN

Location: New-England Psalm-Singer, p.3
          Complete Works: I, p.48
Source of text: Textless   Meter: LM

Tune type: Plain   No. of measures: 17   Key: A
    Time Sig.: 4/4   Incipit: 1323543253143
Reprints by Billings: None   Reprints by others: None

182. NEWBURN

Location: Music in Miniature, p.28
        Complete Works: II, p.316
Source of text: Textless   Meter: LM
Tune type: Plain   No. of measures: 17   Key: E-flat
    Time Sig.: C   Incipit: 5351165651567
Reprints by Billings: None   Reprints by others: None

183. NEWPORT

Location: New-England Psalm-Singer, p.87
        Complete Works: I, p.308
Source of text: Textless   Meter: LM
Tune type: Plain   No. of measures: 16   Key: b
    Time Sig.: 3/4   Incipit: 1565454321357
Reprints by Billings: None   Reprints by others: None

184. NORFOLK

Location: Continental Harmony, p.51
        Complete Works: IV, p.64
Source of text: Watts, Hymns II, No.21   Meter: LM
    First line: Let the old heathens tune their song
Tune type: Twx   No. of measures: 24   Key: E-flat
    Time Sig.: 2/2   Incipit: 5316517654321
Reprints by Billings: None   Reprints by others: None

185. NORTH PROVIDENCE

Location: Singing Master's Assistant, p.71
        Complete Works: II, p.210
Source of text: Watts, Hymns I, no.62   Meter: CM
    First line: Come let us join our cheerful songs
Tune type: Fuging tune   No. of measures: 19   Key: G
    Time Sig.: 2/2   Incipit: 1333212223451
Reprints by Billings: None   Reprints by others: None

Literature: BarbourCM 75

186. NORTH RIVER

Location: New-England Psalm-Singer, p.16
        Complete Works: I, p.96
Source of text: Textless   Meter: CM
Tune type: Plain   No. of measures: 12 Key: a
   Time Sig.: 2/2   Incipit: 1235654553234
Reprints by Billings: None   Reprints by others: None
Literature: BarbourBB 40; BarbourCM 19

187. NORTHBOROUGH

Location: Stickney, Companion, p.41
        Complete Works: III, p.157
Source of text: Anon in KnappNCM, p.162   Meter: PM
   [886886] First line: Behold the splendor, hear the
   shout
Tune type: Fuging tune   No. of measures: 29 Key: F
   Time Sig.: 2/2   Incipit: 5117517111121
Reprints by Billings: 144 17   Reprints by others: 103
   108(var, called HEBRON), 119 145(var, called HEBRON),
   145 160(v)
Notes: Stickney's print called LANESBOROUGH

188. NO. 45

Location: New-England Psalm-Singer, p.79
        Complete Works: I, p.286
Source of text: Textless   Meter: HM
Tune type: Twx   No. of measures: 16 (22) Key: F
   Time Sig.: 3/2 Incipit: 1565455534325
Reprints by Billings: None   Reprints by others: None
Notes: The title is probably a reference to issue No.45
   of John Wilkes's The North Briton (23 April 1763),
   carrying a criticism of a speech by King George III
   that caused Wilkes's arrest for libel. The sobriquet
   "No.45" became a Whig rallying cry in British politics.
Literature: Schrader 414

189. NUTFIELD

Location: New-England Psalm-Singer, p.68
          Complete Works: I, p.244
Source of text: Textless   Meter: SM
Tune type: Plain   No. of measures: 14 Key: e
   Time Sig.: C Incipit: 5553455775655
Reprints by Billings: None   Reprints by others: None

190. OLD BRICK

Location: New-England Psalm-Singer, p.20
          Complete Works: I, p.110
Source of text: Textless   Meter: LM
Tune type: Plain No. of measures: 17 Key: a
   Time Sig.: C Incipit: 1565476554376
Reprints by Billings: None   Reprints by others: None

191. OLD NORTH

Location: New-England Psalm-Singer, p.22
          Complete Works: I, p.118
Source of text: Billings   Meter: SM
   First line: Awake, my soul, awake
Tune type: Twx   No. of measures: 26 Key: F
   Time Sig.: 3/2 Incipit: 1345176551765
Reprints by Billings: None   Reprints by others: None
Notes: Same text used in 146 for AURORA; alternate title:
   MORNING HYMN

192. OLD SOUTH

Location: New-England Psalm-Singer, p.21
          Complete Works: I, p.114
Source of text: Textless   Meter: CM
Tune type: Plain No. of measures: 14 Key: b
   Time Sig.: 4/4 Incipit: 1751235432235
Reprints by Billings: None   Reprints by others: None
Literature: BarbourCM 16

193. ORANGE STREET

Location: New-England Psalm-Singer, p.42
         Complete Works: I, p.162
Source of text: Textless   Meter: CM
Tune type: Plain No. of measures: 14 Key: a
   Time Sig.: 3/2 Incipit: 1171231323557
Reprints by Billings: None   Reprints by others: None

194. ORLEANS

Location: New-England Psalm-Singer, p. 77
         Complete Works: I, p.281
Source of text: Textless   Meter: CM
Tune type: Plain No. of measures: 14   Key: g
   Time Sig.: 3/2 Incipit: 1345654253213
Reprints by Billings: None   Reprints by others: None

195. OXFORD

Location: Music in Miniature, p.27
         Complete Works: II, p.308
Source of text: Textless   Meter: PM [888888]
Tune type: Plain No. of measures: 24 Key: F
   Time Sig.: 2/2 Incipit: 1351717655313
Reprints by Billings: None   Reprints by others: None

196. PARIS

Location: Music in Miniature, p.31
         Complete Works: II, p.326
Source of text: Textless   Meter: LM
Tune type: Plain No. of measures: 16 Key: A
   Time Sig.: 2/2 Incipit: 1123435432113
Reprints by Billings: None   Reprints by others: **10** 70, **21**
   21, **22** 69, **36** 173, **46** 85, **48** 127, **49** 57, **50** 72, **60** 44,
   62 8, **63** 111, **65** 23, **66** 16, **67** 16, **80** 53, **83** 32, **89**
   133, **117** 31, **118** 28, **131** 31, **132** 22, **135** 129, **136** 85,
   150 85, **151** 85, **152** 86, **153** 86, **154** 86, **155** 69, **156** 69,

157 69, **158** 69, **166** 29, **167** 29, **168** 25, **169** 24, **171** 51,
172 16, **173** 60, **178** 101, **179** 101
Recordings: AN

197. PEMBROKE

Location: New-England Psalm-Singer, p.5
          Complete Works: I, p.56
Source of text: Textless (Watts, Hymns I, No.87)
   Meter: LM   First line: Thus saith the high and lofty
   one
Tune type: Plain   No. of measures: 17   Key: D
   Time Sig.: C   Incipit: 1171512327123
Reprints by Billings: None   Reprints by others: None
Notes: Although textless, Billings suggests "Hymn 17"
   (i.e., Hymn 17 in Appendix) as the text. Same text set
   in **112** in CANON 4 IN 1.

198. PEMBROKE NEW

Location: New-England Psalm-Singer, p.10
          Complete Works: I, p.76
Source of text: Textless   Meter: PM [888888]
Tune type: Plain   No. of measures: 24   Key: D
   Time Sig.: 3/2   Incipit: 5153456567651
Reprints by Billings: None   Reprints by others: None

199. PETERSBURGH

Location: Suffolk Harmony, p.28
          Complete Works: III, p.173.
Source of text: Watts, Hymns I, No.87, v.1-2   Meter: LM
   First line: Thus saith the high and lofty one
Tune type: Twx   No. of measures: 42   Key: D
   Time Sig.: 2/4   Incipit: 5111535172727
Reprints by Billings: None   Reprints by others: **22** 28, **42**
   45, **42** 61, **167** 117, **168** 87, **170** 70
Notes: Same text set in **112** in CANON 4 IN 1 and PEMBROKE
Literature: BarbourCM 53

200. PHILADELPHIA

Location: Singing Master's Assistant, p.51
         Complete Works: II, p.172
Source of text: Brady & Tate, Psalm 67, v.3   Meter: SM
   First line: Let diff'ring nations join
Tune type: Fuging chorus No. of measures: 27
   Key: D   Time Sig.: 3/2 and 2/2 intermixed
   Incipit: 5551711543654
Reprints by Billings: 111 20(without fuge)
   Reprints by others: 15 14, 26 46, 27 46, 28 46, 80 56,
   82 32, 106 43, 136 43, 138 44, 140 65, 141 78, 166 69,
   167 69, 168 54, 169 52, 170 37
Literature: BarbourCM 117

201. PHOEBUS

Location: Singing Master's Assistant, p.39
         Complete Works: II, p.148
Source of text: Watts, Psalm 5   Meter: CM
   First line: Lord, in the morning thou shalt hear
Tune type: Twx   No. of measures: 23 Key: f-sharp
   Time Sig.: 2/2 Incipit: 1554345567765
Reprints by Billings: None   Reprints by others: 22 33, 36
   176, 119 24, 123 23, 135 134, 138 37, 180 36
Literature: BarbourCM 85; WienandtBC 36

202. PHYLANTHROPY

Location: Suffolk Harmony, p.36
         Complete Works: III, p.186
Source of text: James Relly, Christian Hymns, Hymn 11
   Meter: PM [8888.10.10]   First line: Jesus, the saviour
   from above
Tune type: Antiphonal Twx   No. of measures: 24 Key: F
   Time Sig.: 2/4 Incipit: 5315671765S:515
Reprints by Billings: None   Reprints by others: None

203. PITT

Location: New-England Psalm-Singer, p.57

Complete Works: I, p.204
Source of text: Textless   Meter: SM
Tune type: Twx   No. of measures: 24 Key: C
  Time Sig.: 2/2 Incipit: 1111711555651
Reprints by Billings: None   Reprints by others: None
Notes: The title is probably a reference to William Pitt,
    a British parliamentarian who advocated consiliatory
    policies and denounced coersive measures toward the
    American colonies.

204. PLAINFIELD

Location: New-England Psalm-Singer, p.93
          Complete Works: I, p.326
Source of text: Textless   Meter: CM
Tune type: Plain   No. of measures: 14 Key: G
  Time Sig.: 3/2 Incipit: 1112531232133
Reprints by Billings: None   Reprints by others: None

205. PLEASANT STREET

Location: New-England Psalm-Singer, p.41
          Complete Works: I, p.156
Source of text: Textless   Meter: LM
Tune type: Plain   No. of measures: 16 Key: a
  Time Sig.: 3/2 Incipit: 1321543123422
Reprints by Billings: None   Reprints by others: None
Manuscripts: MH Ms

206. PLYMOUTH NEW

Location: French, Harmony of Harmony, p.70
          Complete Works: III, p.293
Source of text: Brady & Tate, Psalm 24 (altered),
    v.9, 8 Meter: CM First line: Lift up your heads,
    eternal gates
Tune type: Antiphonal Twx   No. of measures: 38 Key: F
  Time Sig.: 2/2 Incipit: 5671543215432
Reprints by Billings: None   Reprints by others: None
Manuscripts: CtHT-W Ms, MiU-C Ms2, Waterhouse Ms (all T &
    B parts only)

Literature: KroegerWBM 331

207. PLYMTON

Location: New-England Psalm-Singer, p.11
          Complete Works: I, p.78
Source of text: Textless   Meter: PM [888888]
Tune type: Plain No. of measures: 25 Key: b
   Time Sig.: C Incipit: 1132543223454
Reprints by Billings: None   Reprints by others: None

208. POMFRET

Location: New-England Psalm-Singer, p.7
          Complete Works: I, p.66
Source of text: Textless (Brady & Tate, Psalm 92)
   Meter: CM First Line: How good and pleasant must it be
Tune type: Plain No. of measures: 14 Key: G
   Time Sig.: 3/2 Incipit: 1123234565432
Reprints by Billings: None   Reprints by others: None
Notes: Although textless, Billings suggests "Ps.92"
   (i.e., Brady and Tate, Psalm 92) as the text.
Literature: CrawfordMM 586(f)

209. POWNALL

Location: New-England Psalm-Singer, p.67
          Complete Works: I, p.240
Source of text: Textless   Meter: LM
Tune type: Plain No. of measures: 16 Key: a
   Time Sig.: 3/2 Incipit: 1542543223453
Reprints by Billings: None   Reprints by others: None

210. PRINCETOWN

Location: New-England Psalm-Singer, p.45
          Complete Works: I, p.172; II, p.90
Source of text: NEPS: Textless; SMA: Brady & Tate, Psalm
   64 Meter: CM First line: Lord, hear the voice of my
   complaint
Tune type: Plain No. of measures: 14 Key: d

Time Sig.: 3/2   Incipit: 5123211711517
Reprints by Billings: **146** 17(v), **111** 22(v)
Reprints by others: **36** 186, **80** 20, **139** 102(called
PRINCETON)
Notes: **112** & **111** title spelled PRINCE TOWN.

211. PROVIDENCE

Location: New-England Psalm-Singer, p.78
          Complete Works: I, p.282
Source of text: Textless   Meter: LM
Tune type: Plain   No. of measures: 16 Key: e
    Time Sig.: 3/4 Incipit: 1543234517655
Reprints by Billings: None   Reprints by others: None

212. PSALM 18

Location: New-England Psalm-Singer, p.80
          Complete Works: I, p.288
Source of text: Textless (Watts, Psalm 18, Pt.2)
    Meter: CM First Line: To thine almighty arm we owe
Tune type: Twx No. of measures: 16 Key: G
    Time Sig.: 3/2 Incipit: 1543651543253
Reprints by Billings: None   Reprints by others: None
Notes: Billings's title is THE 18TH PSALM. He must have
    intended this tune for a setting of Watts's Psalm 18,
    for the versifications of this Psalm in Sternhold &
    Hopkins, Brady & Tate, and The Bay Psalm Book (the
    three most commonly used versions of the Psalms in
    Billings's day) are in Long Meter.

213. PUMPILY

Location: New-England Psalm-Singer, p.60
          Complete Works: I, p.212; II, p.114
Source of text: Textless (Brady & Tate, Psalm 148)
    Meter: HM First line: Ye boundless realms of joy
Tune type: Twx   No. of measures: NEPS: 13; SMA: 18
    Key: C Time Sig.: NEPS: 3/2; SMA: 2/2
    Incipit: 1312711651322
Reprints by Billings: **146** 24(v), **111** 16(v)

Reprints by others: None
Notes: Although textless, Billings suggests "Psalm 148"
   (i.e., Brady & Tate, Psalm 148) as the text.

214. PURCHASE STREET

 Location: New-England Psalm-Singer, p.73
            Complete Works: I, p.264
 Source of text: Textless   Meter: SM
 Tune type: Plain   No. of measures: 13   Key: F
    Time Sig.: 3/2   Incipit: 1517654556512
 Reprints by Billings: None   Reprints by others: None

215. PURCHASE STREET

 Location: Music in Miniature, p.7
            Complete Works: II, p.296
 Source of text: Textless   Meter: LM
 Tune type: Plain   No. of measures: 16   Key: E-flat
    Time Sig.: 3/2   Incipit: 5517656567117
 Reprints by Billings: None   Reprints by others: None

216. QUEEN STREET

 Location: New-England Psalm-Singer, p.50
            Complete Works: I, p.188
 Source of text: Perez Morton   Meter: CM
    First line: O clap your hands and shout for joy
 Tune type: Twx   No. of measures: 17   Key: F
    Time Sig.: 2/2   Incipit: 1553312345517
 Reprints by Billings: None   Reprints by others: None
 Notes: The same text is used for ANTHEM: O Clap Your Hands
    (Ind Pub; Complete Works III, p.252).

217. RALEIGH

 Location: Couch, Northwestern Harmony, p.66
            Complete Works: III, p.333
 Source of text: Watts, Psalm 17, v.6   Meter: LM
    First line: My flesh shall slumber in the ground
 Tune type: Plain   No. of Measures: 16   Key: d

Time Sig.: 2/2   Incipit: 1555577771111
Reprints by Billings: None   Reprints by others: **109** 42
Notes: It is doubtful that this tune is by Billings, but
its ascription to him in Couch's Ms tunebook and **109**
cannot be disproven.

218. REDEMPTION

Location: Psalm-Singer's Amusement, p.22
          Complete Works: III, p.32
Source of text: Anon in KnappNCM, p.164   Meter: PM
   [8868886] First line: Th'eternal speaks, all heav'n
   attends
Tune type: Fuging tune No. of measures: 34 Key: E-flat
   Time Sig.: 2/2   Incipit: 5311716553143
Reprints by Billings: None   Reprints by others: **9** 20, **36**
   158, **61** 50, **90** 149(v), **105** 66, **135** 143
Literature: KroegerWP 50

219. RESIGNATION

Location: Psalm-Singer's Amusement, p.62
          Complete Works: III, p.82
Source of text: Watts, Hymns II, No.83   Meter: CM
   First line: Thus saith the ruler of the skies
Tune type: Twx No. of measures: 31 Key: e
   Time Sig.: 3/2; 2/2 Incipit: 5565176545551
Reprints by Billings: None   Reprints by others: None
Literature: KroegerWP 53,

220. RESTORATION

Location: Suffolk Harmony, p.35
          Complete Works: III, p.183
Source of text: James Relly, Christian Hymns, Hymn 5
   Meter: PM [4446624446]   First line: Greatly beloved,
   Of God approv'd
Tune type: Twx No. of measures: 23 Key: D
   Time Sig.: 2/4 Incipit: 5555155567176
Reprints by Billings: None   Reprints by others: None

221. RESURRECTION

Location: Independent Publication (1787), p.7
         Complete Works: III, p.234
Source of text: Anon. in Lyra Davidica   Meter: PM [7777
   with Hallelujah refrain]   First line: Jesus Christ is
   ris'n today, Hallelujah
Tune type: Twx   No. of measures: 20 Key: C
   Time Sig.: 6/4 Incipit: 5512321176517
Reprints by Billings: None   Reprints by others: None
Notes: The 1st, 3d, and 5th Hallelujah refrains were taken
   from Billings's anthem, PEACE (1783), mm.86-95.
   Tunename followed by the note: "for Easter."

222. REVELATION

Location: Music in Miniature, p.29
         Complete Works: II, p.320
Source of text: Textless Meter: CM
Tune type: Plain   No. of measures: 15 Key: a
   Time Sig.: 2/2 Incipit: 1123234553212
Reprints by Billings: 31 62(as Fuging chorus)
   Reprints by others: 72 11

223. REVELATION

Location: Continental Harmony, p.62
         Complete Works: IV, p.87
Source of Text: Watts, Psalm 119, Pt.7 Meter: CM
   First line: Let all the heathen writers join
Tune type: Fuging chorus No. of measures: 35 Key: a
   Time Sig.: 2/2; 3/2 Incipit: 1123234553212
Reprints by Billings: None Reprints by others: None
Notes: printed in 111 29 as Plain tune.

224. RICHMOND

Location: Singing Master's Assistant, p.50
         Complete Works: II, p.170

Source of text: James Relly, Christian Hymns, Hymn 55
    Meter: PM [787877] First line: My beloved haste away
Tune type: Twx verse and chorus   No. of measures: 16
    Key: a   Time Sig.: 6/4; 2/4 Incipit: 1512354321321
Reprints by Billings: 144 23   Reprints by others: 52 99,
    53 99, 87 57, 106 12, 119 181, 136 12, 137 61, 145 61
Recordings: E

225. ROCHESTER

Location: Continental Harmony, p.81
          Complete Works: IV, p.120
Source of text: Charles Wesley, in Whitefield Collection,
    Hymn 50 Meter: PM [5556565]   First line: Ye servants
    of God, your master proclaim
Tune type: Antiphonal Twx   No. of measures: 9 Key: C
    Time Sig.: 6/4 Incipit: 1345134321S:517
Reprints by Billings: None   Reprints by others: None
Literature: BarbourCM 98

226. ROCKY-NOOK

Location: Continental Harmony, p.49
          Complete Works: IV, p.58
Source of text: Watts, Hymns I, No.41   Meter: CM
    First line: Those glorious minds, how bright they shine
Tune type: Fuging tune   No. of measures: 18 Key: G
    Time Sig.: 2/2 Incipit: 1323543215654
Reprints by Billings: None   Reprints by others: 89 141,
    90 152

227. ROXBURY

Location: New-England Psalm-Singer, p.20
          Complete Works: I, p.112
Source of text: Textless   Meter: LM
Tune type: Plain   No. of measures: 16 Key: a
    Time Sig.: 3/2 Incipit: 1345456765432
Reprints by Billings: None   Reprints by others: None

228. ROXBURY

Location: Singing Master's Assistant, p.46
        Complete Works: II, p.162
Source of text: Brady & Tate, Psalm 149   Meter: PM
  [55556565] First line: O praise ye the Lord, Prepare
  your glad voice
Tune type: Plain No. of measures: 16 Key: D
  Time Sig.: 3/4 Incipit: 5517176511711
Reprints by Billings: 111 24 Reprints by others: None

229. RUTLAND

Location: Psalm-Singer's Amusement, p.48
        Complete Works: III, p.62
Source of text: Watts, Psalm 17, v.6, 4   Meter: LM
  First line: My flesh shall slumber in the ground
Tune type: Set Piece No. of measures: 78 Key: a; d; C
  Time Sig.: 2/2; 3/4; 2/2 Incipit: B:155654345T:1551
Reprints by Billings: None   Reprints by others: None
Literature: KroegerST 21

230. ST. ANDREWS

Location: Continental Harmony, p.184
        Complete Works: IV, p.274
Source of text: Watts, Hymns I, No.1   Meter: CM
  First line: Behold the glories of the lamb
Tune type: Fuging chorus No. of measures: 21 Key: C
  Time Sig.: 2/2 Incipit: 1551432171512
Reprints by Billings: None   Reprints by others: None

231. ST. ELISHA'S

Location: New-England Psalm-Singer, p.8
        Complete Works: I, p.68
Source of text: Textless (Watts, Hymns I, No.67)
  Meter: LM First line: Thou whom my soul admires above
Tune type: Plain No. of measures: 16 Key: D

Time Sig.: 3/2 Incipit: 1565432345327
Reprints by Billings: None   Reprints by others: None
Notes: Although textless, Billings suggests "Hymn 14"
    (i.e., Hymn 14 in Appendix) as the text, which is
    Watts, Hymns I, No.67.

232. ST. ENOCH

Location: Continental Harmony, p.67
         Complete Works: IV, p.96
Source of text: Brady & Tate, Psalm 98   Meter: CM
    First line: Sing to the Lord a new made song
Tune type: Fuging tune   No. of measures: 25 Key: C
    Time Sig.: 2/2 Incipit: 1343434342323
Reprints by Billings: None   Reprints by others: None
Notes: Note at head: "For a Thanksgiving, after a Victory"
Literature: BarbourCM 65

233. ST. JOHN'S

Location: Continental Harmony, p.55
         Complete Works: IV, p.72
Source of text: Watts, Hymns II, No.154   Meter: LM
    First line: Where are the mourners, saith the Lord
Tune type: Plain   No. of measures: 17 Key: g
    Time Sig.: 2/2 Incipit: 1123454354321
Reprints by Billings: None   Reprints by others: **180
100**

234. ST. PETER'S

Location: Pilsbury, United States' Sacred Harmony,
         p.118   Complete Works: III, p.296
Source of text: Charles Wesley, Hymns(1749)   Meter: PM
    [8888 anapestic] First line: How shall a lost sinner
    in pain
Tune type: Twx   No. of measures: 14. Key: c
    Time Sig.: 2/2 Incipit: 5171232122321
Reprints by Billings: None   Reprints by others: **52** 91, **53**
    91
Notes: Ascribed to Billings on the basis of its being a

variant of SAVANNAH (146 3)

235. ST. THOMAS

Location: Continental Harmony, p.127
           Complete Works: IV, p.187
Source of text: Watts, Hymns II, No.95, v.1,4-5
   Meter: CM First line: Methinks I see my saviour dear
Tune type: Twx No. of measures: 47 Key: c
   Time Sig.: 3/2; 2/2; 3/2; 2/2 Incipit: 5171235432115
Reprints by Billings: 111 29(first 15 m. as CALVARY)
   Reprints by others: 76 27(first 15 m. only)
Notes: Note at bottom: "Observe that this tune will
   contain four verses." First stanza of text is not by
   Watts and is unlocated (also found in 123, p.26 in
   CRUCIFIXION by Harris).

236. ST. VINCENT'S

Location: Sacred Harmony (ca.1788), p.98
           Complete Works: III, p.298
Source of text: Watts, Hymns I, No.9   Meter: CM
   First line: In vain we lavish out our lives
Tune type: Plain No. of measures: 14 Key: a
   Time Sig.: 3/4 Incipit: 1543232171232
Reprints by Billings: None   Reprints by others: 55 54(v)
Notes: Ascribed to Billings on the basis of its being a
   variant of CONCORD (112 5)

237. SAPPHO

Location: New-England Psalm-Singer, p.108
           Complete Works: I, p.355, II, p.105
Source of text: Watts, Horae Lyricae, "The Day of
   Judgment" Meter: PM [11.11.11.5] First line: When the
   fierce north wind with his airy forces
Tune type: Twx No. of measures: NEPS: 22 (29); SMA: 23
   Key: C   Time Sig.: NEPS: 3/2; SMA: 2/2
   Incipit: 1171543212345
Reprints by Billings: 146 21(v)   Reprints by others: 36

169, **135** 146(v), **149** 47(v), **180** 118(v)
Manuscripts: MSaE Ms1, MWA Ms
Notes: Title in **111**: A New Tune to Dr. Watts's Sapphick
Ode by W B.

238. SAVANNAH

Location: Singing Master's Assistant, p. 3
           Complete Works: II, p.44
Source of text: Charles Wesley, in Whitefield Collection,
    Hymn 48   Meter: PM [8888 anapestic]
    First line: Ah, lovely appearance of death
Tune type: Antiphonal Plain   No. of measures: 14   Key: c
    Time Sig.: 2/2   Incipit: 5112321223212
Reprints by Billings: None   Reprints by others: **37** 37,
    89 151, **90** 158, **135** 147, **145** 145, **176** 56, **177** 46, **180**
    127
Manuscripts: MiU-C Ms1
Notes: Billings attributes the text to G. Whitefield. ST.
    PETER'S in **117** 118 is a variant.
Literature: BarbourCM 125

239. SAYBROOK

Location: Music in Miniature, p.30
           Complete Works: II, p.324
Source of text: Textless   Meter: LM
Tune type: Plain   No. of measures: 20   Key: g
    Time Sig.: 2/2   Incipit: 1543232132323
Reprints by Billings: None   Reprints by others: None
Notes: DUNSTABLE in MHi Ms is a variant

240. SCITUATE

Location: New-England Psalm-Singer, p.9
           Complete Works: I, p.72
Source of text: Textless   Meter: LM
Tune type: Plain   No. of measures: 16   Key: b
    Time Sig.: 3/2   Incipit: 1123234543432
Reprints by Billings: None   Reprints by others: None
Literature: NathanWB 20(f)

241. SHARON

Location: Singing Master's Assistant, p.32
         Complete Works: II, p.133
Source of text: Watts, Divine Songs, No.1   Meter: CM
  First line: How glorious is our heav'nly king
Tune type: Twx   No. of measures: 16   Key: G
  Time Sig.: 6/4; 3/2   Incipit: 1133234535646
Reprints by Billings: None   Reprints by others: None
Literature: BarbourCM 38

242. SHEFFIELD

Location: Huntington, Apollo Harmony, p.48
         Complete Works: III, p.301
Source of text: Watts, Psalm 98, Pt.2, v.1-2 Meter: CM
  First line: Joy to the world, the Lord is come
Tune type: Double Fuging tune   No. of measures: 26
  Key: A   Time Sig.: 2/2   Incipit: 1132234553143
Reprints by Billings: None   Reprints by others: 34 25(v),
  77 14, 89 166, 147 47
Manuscripts: Cowling 10(unattributed)
Notes: It is doubtful that this tune is actually by
  Billings, but no other attributions have been found.

243. SHERBURNE

Location: Singing Master's Assistant, p.43
         Complete Works: II, p.156
Source of text: Watts, Psalm 133   Meter: PM [668668]
  First line: How pleasant 'tis to see
Tune type: Plain.   No. of measures: 15   Key: F
  Time Sig.: 2/2   Incipit: 1556711171765
Reprints by Billings: 111 12(v)   Reprints by others: 18
  44, 32 17(called DUBLIN NEW), 33 17(called DUBLIN NEW),
  76 91, 80 31, 104 42

244. SHILOH

Location: Suffolk Harmony, p.1
         Complete Works: III, p.138

Source of text: Billings   Meter: CM
   First line: Methinks I see an heav'nly host
Tune type: Antiphonal verse and chorus
   No. of measures: 22 Key: G   Time Sig.: 2/2; 6/4
   Incipit: 5111233334556
Reprints by Billings: None   Reprints by others: None
Notes: Note at head: "for Christmas." The complete
   10-stanza text given on facing page. First 2 stanzas
   also used for BOSTON in 146.
Literature: BarbourCM 46; KroegerWBHT 23; McKay 141;
   NathanWB(f); Stevenson 65
Recordings: N, R, AD

245. SHIRLEY

Location: New-England Psalm-Singer, p.74
             Complete Works: I, p.268
Source of text: Textless   Meter: LM
Tune type: Plain   No. of measures: 17   Key: e
   Time Sig.: C Incipit: 1534534253422
Reprints by Billings: None   Reprints by others: None
Notes: LANCASTER (112 43) is a transposed version

246. SINAI

Location: Suffolk Harmony, p.45
             Complete Works: III, p.200
Source of text: James Relly, Christian Hymns, Hymn 69
   Meter: PM [888888] First line: All you who make the
   law your choice
Tune type: Twx verse and chorus No. of measures: 21
   Key: d   Time Sig.: 3/2; 2/2 Incipit: 5534754554457
Reprints by Billings: None   Reprints by others: 60 98,
   63 63

247. SMITHFIELD

Location: New-England Psalm-Singer, p.92
             Complete Works: I, p.322
Source of text: Brady & Tate, Psalm 15   Meter: CM
   First line: Lord, who's the happy man that may

Tune type: Antiphonal verse and chorus
   No. of measures: 22   Key: a   Time Sig.: 3/2
   Incipit: B:11756717651T:51
Reprints by Billings: None   Reprints by others: None

248. SOUTH-BOSTON

 Location: Continental Harmony, p.83
          Complete Works: IV, p. 124
 Source of text: Watts, Hymns I, No.150   Meter: HM
    First line: Join all the glorious names
 Tune type: Twx   No. of measures: 16   Key: C
    Time Sig.: 2/2   Incipit: 5112321132343
 Reprints by Billings: None   Reprints by others: None

249. SPAIN

 Location: Singing Master's Assistant, p.42
          Complete Works: II, p.154
 Source of text: Watts, Psalm 122   Meter: PM [668668]
    First line: How pleas'd and blest was I
 Tune type: Plain   No. of measures: 22   Key: C
    Time Sig.: 2/2   Incipit: 1134322354211
 Reprints by Billings: **111** 13   Reprints by others: None

250. SPENCER

 Location: Waterhouse Ms, p.7
          Complete Works: III, p.334
 Source of text: Textless   Meter: CM
 Tune type: Plain   No. of measures: 14   Key: G
    Time Sig.: 3/2   Incipit: 1171235443143
 Reprints by Billings: None   Reprints by others: None
 Notes: Ascribed to Billings on the basis of its being a
    variant of BOLTON
 Literature: KroegerWBM 339

251. STOCKBRIDGE

 Location: Singing Master's Assistant, p.44
          Complete Works: II, p.159

Source of text: Watts, Psalm 117, v.1; Brady & Tate, Psalm
    95, v.1-2,6 Meter: LM First line: Watts: From all
    that dwell below the skies; B&T: O come, loud anthems
    let us sing
Tune type: Antiphonal Twx   No. of measures: 38 Key: F
    Time Sig.: 2/2 Incipit: B:11765671T:55432
Reprints by Billings: None   Reprints by others: **36** 118,
    46 93, **63** 65(ends at m.18), **80** 42, **87** 16(v), **106**
    15(ends at m.28), **136** 15(v), **145** 190, **150** 31(ends at
    m.18), **150** 36(complete), **151** 31(ends at m.18), **151**
    36(complete), **152** 36(v), **166** 30, **167** 30
Manuscripts: MiU-C Ms1 (v), NN Ms (v)
Literature: BarbourCM 18; KroegerWBHT 23

252. STOUGHTON

Location: New-England Psalm-Singer, p.42
         Complete Works: I, p.160
Source of text: Textless   Meter: CM
Tune type: Plain   No. of measures: 14 Key: A
    Time Sig.: 3/4 Incipit: 1345321234542
Reprints by Billings: None   Reprints by others: None

253. STURBRIDGE

Location: Music in Miniature, p.5
         Complete Works: II, p.288
Source of text: Textless   Meter: LM
Tune type: Plain No. of measures: 16 Key: G
    Time Sig.: 3/2 Incipit: 1534231555345
Reprints by Billings: None Reprints by others: None

254. SUDBURY

Location: New-England Psalm-Singer, p.12
         Complete Works: I, p.82
Source of text: Textless   Meter: CM
Tune type: Plain No. of measures: 15   Key: F
    Time Sig.: 2/2 Incipit: 1515645313465
Reprints by Billings: None   Reprints by others: None

255. SUDBURY

Location: Continental Harmony, p.69
          Complete Works: IV, p.100
Source of text: John Peck, "On the Resurrection," in
    Description, v.1-2   Meter: SM   First line: What if a
    saint must die
Tune type: Antiphonal Twx   No. of measures: 17   Key: C
    Time Sig.: 6/4   Incipit: 5171321765125
Reprints by Billings: None   Reprints by others: **107**
    145(called WEST SUDBURY), **108** 145(called WEST SUDBURY),
    109 139(called WEST-SUDBURY)
Notes: called WEST SUDBURY on score, but corrected to
    SUDBURY in index.
Literature: BarbourCM 125

256. SUFFOLK

Location: New-England Psalm-Singer, p.17
          Complete Works: I, p.100; II, p.92
Source of text: NEPS: Textless; SMA: Watts, Hymns II,
    No.51   Meter: LM   First line: Bright king of glory,
    dreadful God
Tune type: Plain   No. of measures: 16   Key: g
    Time Sig.: 3/2   Incipit: 1517654512345
Reprints by Billings: **146** 17(v), **111** 25(v)
    Reprints by others: **22** 64(in F# minor), **36** 171, **48** 129,
    49 59(in F# minor), **57** 53, **60** 51, **68** 349, **103** 38, **104**
    13, **119** 76, **136** 86, **138** 20, **139** 102, **166** 39, **167** 39,
    168 30, **169** 31, **170** 55, **171** 51
Manuscripts: DLC Ms (**112** version without bass octaves)
    possibly dating from 1767

257. SULLIVAN

Location: Singing Master's Assistant, p.9
          Complete Works: II, p.62
Source of text: Watts, Hymns I, No.58   Meter: LM
    First line: Let mortal tongues attempt to sing
Tune type: Plain   No. of measures: 16   Key: D

Time Sig.: 3/2   Incipit: 5517176512171
Reprints by Billings: None   Reprints by others: None

258. SUMMER STREET

Location: New-England Psalm-Singer, p.66
          Complete Works: I, p.238
Source of text: Textless   Meter: CM
Tune type: Plain   No. of measures: 14 Key: a
   Time Sig.: 3/2   Incipit: 1321512345654
Reprints by Billings: None   Reprints by others: None

259. SUNDAY

Location: Singing Master's Assistant, p.54
          Complete Works: II, p.178
Source of text: Billings   Meter: LM
   First line: Majestic God, when I descry
Tune type: Twx   No. of measures: 23
   Key: E-flat   Time Sig.: 3/2and 2/2 intermixed
   Incipit: 5132715315517
Reprints by Billings: None   Reprints by others: None
Notes: Same text used for BRIDGWATER in **112**
Literature: BarbourCM 39, KroegerWP 43

260. SWANZEY

Location: New-England Psalm-Singer, p.72
          Complete Works: I, p.260
Source of text: Textless   Meter: CM
Tune type: Plain   No. of measures: 14 Key: a
   Time Sig.: 3/2   Incipit: 1543217123555
Reprints by Billings: None   Reprints by others: None

261. TAUNTON

Location: New-England Psalm-Singer, p.49
          Complete Works: I, p.185
Source of text: Brady & Tate, Psalm 42   Meter: CM
   First line: As pants the hart for cooling streams

Tune type: Fuging chorus   No. of measures: 30   Key: a
    Time Sig.: 3/2   Incipit: 1545432343223
Reprints by Billings: None   Reprints by others: None

262. THOMAS-TOWN

Location: Continental Harmony, p.66
          Complete Works: IV, p.94
Source of text: Mather Byles, Poems, v.1,13   Meter: CM
    First line: Great God, how frail a thing is man
Tune type: Twx   No. of measures: 20   Key: g
    Time Sig.: 2/2   Incipit: 1171234556543
Reprints by Billings: None   Reprints by others: 9 88
    (called DEERFIELD), 70 18, 72 2(v), 89 168(var, called
    THOMASTON), 103 50(called DEERFIELD), 105 19(called
    DEERFIELD), 122 2(v)
Manuscripts: MHi Ms (called DEEARFIELD), NN Ms (incompl.,
    m.11-20 only)

263. TOWER HILL

Location: New-England Psalm-Singer, p.58
          Complete Works: I, p.208
Source of text: Textless   Meter: CM
Tune type: Plain   No. of measures: 14   Key: a
    Time Sig.: 3/2   Incipit: 1135754557534
Reprints by Billings: None.   Reprints by others: None

264. TRINITY-NEW

Location: Music in Miniature, p.32
          Complete Works: II, p.334
Source of text: Textless   Meter: CM
Tune type: Plain   No. of measures: 14   Key: E
    Time Sig.: 3/2   Incipit: 5165651711176
Reprints by Billings: None   Reprints by others: None

265. UNION

Location: New-England Psalm-Singer, p.4
          Complete Works: I, p.54

Source of text: Textless (Brady & Tate, Psalm 25)
    Meter: SM   First line: To God, in whom I trust
Tune type: Plain   No. of measures: 13   Key: C
    Time Sig.: 3/2   Incipit: 5154321234565
Reprints by Billings: None   Reprints by others: None
Notes: Although textless, Billings suggests "Ps.25" (i.e.,
    Brady & Tate, Psalm 25) as the text.
Literature: BarbourCM 50

266. UNION

Location: Worcester Collection, 2d ed., p.118
            Complete Works: III, p.304
Source of text: Watts, Psalm 148, v.1-3   Meter: LM
    First line: Loud hallelujahs to the Lord
Tune type: Antiphonal Twx   No. of measures: 59
    Key: E-flat   Time Sig.: 2/4   Incipit: 5671117654321
Reprints by Billings: None   Reprints by others: 46 21, 47
    54, 48 54, 150 92, 151 92, 168 88
Manuscripts: Rutgers Ms 1
Notes: Attributed to Billings in 168, but not in 167.

267. UNITY

Location: New-England Psalm-Singer, p.18
            Complete Works: I, p.104
Source of text: Textless   Meter: LM
Tune type: Plain   No. of measures: 17   Key: D
    Time Sig.: C   Incipit: 1151432151342
Reprints by Billings: None   Reprints by others: None

268. UXBRIDGE

Location: New-England Psalm-Singer, p.64
            Complete Works: I, p.228; III, p.308
Source of text: Textless   Meter: CM
Tune type: Plain   No. of measures: 14   Key: G
    Time Sig.: 3/4   Incipit: 1543512343215
Reprints by Billings: None   Reprints by others: 54
    8(var., called LESSON VI)

269. VERMONT

Location: Singing Master's Assistant, p.55
           Complete Works: II, p.180
Source of text: Watts, Hymns I, No.9   Meter: CM
   First line: In vain we lavish out our lives
Tune type: Twx   No. of measures: 18 Key: e
   Time Sig.: 2/2 Incipit: 5315171765434
Reprints by Billings: None   Reprints by others: 36 71,
   43 41, 83 73, 135 164(v), 180 19
Literature: BarbourCM 87

270. VICTORY

Location: Continental Harmony, p.170
           Complete Works: IV, p.254
Source of text: Watts, Psalm 18, Pt.2   Meter: CM
   First line: To thine almighty arm we owe
Tune type: Antiphonal Twx   No. of measures: 25
   Key: B-flat   Time Sig.: 2/2 Incipit: 5123454543214
Reprints by Billings: None   Reprints by others: None
Manuscripts: Waterhouse Ms(T & B only, in B major), MiU-C
   Ms2 106(var, T & B only, in B major)

271. WALTHAM

Location: New-England Psalm-Singer, p.95
           Complete Works: I, p.332; II, p.100
Source of text: NEPS: Perez Morton; SMA: Watts, Psalm 45
   Meter: SM First line: NEPS: To thee I made my cry;
   SMA: My Saviour and my king
Tune type: Plain   No. of measures: 13 Key: C
   Time Sig.: 3/2 Incipit: 5123214322156
Reprints by Billings: 146 20(v); 111 10(v)
   Reprints by others: 22 37, 36 159, 76 78
Notes: BEDFORD in 136 is a variant

272. WAREHAM

Location: Music in Miniature, p.31
           Complete Works: II, p.328

Source of text: Textless   Meter: SM
Tune type: Plain   No. of measures: 10   Key: a
   Time Sig.: 2/2   Incipit: 1123454321235
Reprints by Billings: **121** 51(as Fuging chorus)
   Reprints by others: None

273. WAREHAM

Location: Psalm-Singer's Amusement, p.51
          Complete Works: III, p.67
Source of text: Watts, Hymns II, No.93   Meter: SM
   First line: My God, my life, my love
Tune type: Fuging chorus   No. of measures: 37   Key: a
   Time Sig.: 2/2   Incipit: 1123454321235
Reprints by Billings: **111** 31 (as Plain tune)
   Reprints by others: None

274. WARREN

Location: Singing Master's Assistant, p.62
          Complete Works: II, p.193
Source of text: John Cennick, in Whitefield Collection,
   Hymn 38   Meter: PM [7777]   First line: Children of
   the heav'nly king
Tune type: Twx   No. of measures: 8   Key: G
   Time Sig.: 6/8   Incipit: 1212345432143
Reprints by Billings: None   Reprints by others: **44** 47, **52**
   63, **53** 63, **81** 21, **82** 45
Notes: Billings attributes the text to G. Whitefield.

275. WASHINGTON

Location: Singing Master's Assistant, p.79
          Complete Works: II, p.227
Source of text: Watts, Psalm 68   Meter: LM
   First line: Lord, when thou didst ascend on high
Tune type: Fuging tune   No. of measures: 27   Key: E
   Time Sig.: 2/2   Incipit: 5551712321765
Reprints by Billings: None   Reprints by others: **1** 10, **2**

10, 3 10, 4 30, 5 30, 6 30, 15 36, 21 38, 26 30, 27 30,
28 30, 32 48, 33 48, 78 48, 80 24, 84 30, 117 47, 133
87, 134 70, 135 16, 137 26, 138 31, 142 70, 162 34,
163 34, 164 28(v), 165 29
Literature: Hamm 145; KroegerST 24
Recordings: E, M

276. WASHINGTON-STREET

Location: Continental Harmony, p.64
          Complete Works: IV, p.91
Source of text: Watts, Hymns I, No.39   Meter: CM
   First line: Now shall my inward joys arise
Tune type: Fuging chorus   No. of measures: 27 Key: F
   Time Sig.: 2/2 Incipit: 1556677176543
Reprints by Billings: None   Reprints by others: None

277. WATER TOWN

Location: New-England Psalm-Singer, p.13
          Complete Works: I, p.84
Source of text: Textless Meter: LM
Tune type: Plain No. of measures: 17 Key: D
   Time Sig.: 3/4 Incipit: 5517154654322
Reprints by Billings: None Reprints by others: None

278. WELLFLEET

Location: New-England Psalm-Singer, p.61
          Complete Works: I, p.218
Source of text: Textless   Meter: SM
Tune type: Plain   No. of measures: 13 Key: a
   Time Sig.: 3/2 Incipit: 1534213543213
Reprints by Billings: None   Reprints by others: None

279. WEST BOSTON

Location: Suffolk Harmony, p.41
          Complete Works: III, p.194
Source of text: John Relly, Christian Hymns, Hymn 28.

v.1-2   Meter: PM [7777] First line: Come, ye lovers
of the lamb
Tune type: Twx verse and chorus   No. of measures: 25
   Key: d   Time Sig.: 2/4; 6/4 Incipit: 5511232171765
Reprints by Billings: None   Reprints by others: 47 124,
   48 54

280. WEST-SUDBURY

Location: Continental Harmony, p.50
         Complete Works: IV, p.61
Source of text: John Peck, "A Poem on Death," in
   Description, v.1-2   Meter: CM   First line: Here is a
   song which doth belong
Tune type: Twx   No. of measures: 21 Key: f-sharp
   Time Sig.: 2/2 Incipit: 1345654321234
Reprints by Billings: None.   Reprints by others: **53**
   47(v)

281. WESTFIELD

Location: New-England Psalm-Singer, p.71
         Complete Works: I, p.254
Source of text: Textless   Meter: LM
Tune type: Plain   No. of measures: 16 Key: f-sharp
   Time Sig.: 3/2 Incipit: 1154371567655
Reprints by Billings: None   Reprints by others: None

282. WEYMOUTH

Location: Continental Harmony, p.74
         Complete Works: IV, p.109
Source of text: Watts, Hymns I, No.106   Meter: SM
   First line: Shall we go on to sin
Tune type: Fuging chorus   No. of measures: 33 Key: g
   Time Sig.: 3/2; 2/2 Incipit: 1345432123215
Reprints by Billings: None   Reprints by others: None
Manuscripts: Waterhouse Ms 5(T & B only), MiU-C Ms2
   113(var, T & B only), MHi Ms
Notes: LEXINGTON (**112** 66) is possibly an earlier
   version.

283. WHEELER'S POINT

Location: Suffolk Harmony, p.21
          Complete Works: III, p.165
Source of text: Brady & Tate, Psalm 126   Meter: CM
   First line: When Sion's God her sons recall'd
Tune type: Fuging chorus   No. of measures: 30 Key: a
   Time Sig.: 3/2; 2/2 Incipit: 1543234535432
Reprints by Billings: None   Reprints by others: 71 4(v),
   72 12(v), 145 150(var, called DARTMOUTH)

284. WHEELLER'S POINT

Location: New-England Psalm-Singer, p.18
          Complete Works: I, p.102
Source of text: Textless   Meter: LM
Tune type: Plain   No. of measures: 16 Key: d
   Time Sig.: 3/2 Incipit: 1345171543223
Reprints by Billings: None   Reprints by others: None

285. WILKS

Location: New-England Psalm-Singer, p.80
          Complete Works: I, p.290
Source of text: Perez Morton   Meter: LM
   First line: Almighty God, eternal king
Tune type: Plain   No. of measures: 16 Key: D
   Time Sig.: 3/2 Incipit: 1176515432115
Reprints by Billings: None   Reprints by others: None
Notes: The title is probably a reference to John Wilkes,
   a champion of free speech and the rights of the
   American colonies in the British parliament. (See also
   note for NO.45, above.)
Literature: Schrader 415

286. WILLIAMSBURGH

Location: New-England Psalm-Singer, p.87
          Complete Works: I, p.311
Source of text: Billings?   Meter: CM
   First line: Almighty God whose boundless sway

Tune type: Plain   No. of measures: 15   Key: G
   Time Sig.: 3/2 Incipit: 1343456543432
Reprints by Billings: None   Reprints by others: None

287. WORCESTER

Location: Singing Master's Assistant, p.48
           Complete Works: II, p.166
Source of text: Watts, Hymns II, No.32   Meter: CM
   First line: How short and hasty are our lives
Tune type: Twx   No. of measures: 19 Key: g
   Time Sig.: 2/2 Incipit: 1323543212354
Reprints by Billings: None   Reprints by others: 120 33

288. WRENTHAM

Location: Singing Master's Assistant, p.28
      Complete Works: II, p.122
Source of text: Watts, Psalm 50   Meter: PM
   [10.10.10.10.11.11] First line: The God of glory sends
   his summons forth
Tune type: Plain   No. of measures: 26 Key: F
   Time Sig.: 2/2 Incipit: 1355535432534
Reprints by Billings: 111 15   Reprints by others: 32 53,
   33 53, 80 16, 104 44, 105 55, 131 70, 132 55, 139 89,
   167 53
Literature: KroegerSIWP 21

ANTHEMS

289. And I Saw A Mighty Angel

Billings's Title: An Anthem. Revns Chap. 5th
Location: Psalm-Singer's Amusement, p.35-45
          Complete Works: III, p.46-57
Source of text: Bible, Authorized Version, Revelation
    5:2-8,12,9-10; Revelation 4:8; Revelation 15:3; with
    Billings's additions and alterations.
No. of meas: 258   Key: B; b; B   Time Sig.: 2/2; 2/4
    Directive words: m.30 Affetuoso Incipit: 1512323455432
    Timing: 5:00
Reprints by Billings: None   Reprints by others: **55** 76,
    122 35, **126** 25

290. As The Hart Panteth

Billings's Title: An Anthem Psalm 42
Location: New-England Psalm-Singer, p.31-39
          Complete Works: I, p.138-151
Source of text: Bible, Authorized Version, Psalm 42, with
    Billings's additions and alterations.

No. of meas: 217   Key: g; G; g; G   Time Sig.: 4/4; 2/2;
2/4; C; 3/2; C; 2/2; 3/2; C; 3/2; C
Directive words: m.88 Vivace; m.105 Gravisonos; m.127
Adagio; m.169 Vigoroso; m.197 Adagio; m.214 Adagio
Incipit: B:17151237321T:55   Timing: 15:22
Reprints by Billings: None   Reprints by others: None
Literature: Daniel 229
Recordings: H

291. Behold How Good And Joyful

Billings's Title: UNION. An Anthem. Ps. 133
Location: Suffolk Harmony p.3-9
         Complete Works: III, p.141-147
Source of text: Bible, Psalms, Common Prayer version,
Psalm 133:1-4; Doxology by Thomas Ken; with Billings's
additions and alterations.
No. of meas: 83   Key: C   Time Sig.: 3/2 and 2/2
intermixed   Directive words: None   Incipit:
512123453112   Timing: 5:21
Reprints by Billings: None   Reprints by others: None

292. Blessed Is He That Considereth The Poor

Billings's Title: Suitable to be sung at a Charity
meeting. Anthem taken from Mathew 5 & 25 1 Chorin
Chap 13 & 14 Psalm 34 & 41.
Location: New-England Psalm-Singer, p.97-107
         Complete Works: I, p.340-353
Source of text: Bible, Authorized Version, Psalm 41:1-2;
Matthew 5:7; I Corinthians 14:1, 13:13; Psalm 41:3;
Psalm 34:6; Matthew 25:34-35; Psalm 41:13; with
Billings's additions and alterations
No. of meas: 141 (182)   Key: C; c; C; c; C
Time Sig.: 3/2, 4/4, 3/4, 2/4, and C intermixed
Directive words: m.1 Largo; m.35 Maestuso; m.60
Affetuoso; m.68 Adagio; m.72 Vigoroso; m.89
Languissiant; m.96 Presto; m.127 Vivace; m.136 Grave;
m.139 Adagio   Incipit: 1323234321251   Timing: 9:25
Reprints by Billings: None   Reprints by others: None

293. Blessed Is He That Considereth The Poor

Billings's Title: An Anthem taken from sundry Scriptures
    for Charity meetings.
Location: Psalm-Singer's Amusement, p.24-35
        Complete Works: III, p.35-45
Source of text: Bible, Authorized Version, Psalm 41:1-2;
    Matthew 5:7; I Corinthians 14:1, 13:13; Psalm 41:3;
    Proverbs 19:17; Psalm 34:6; Psalm 68:6; James 1:27;
    Psalm 106:48; with Billings's additions and
    alterations.
No. of meas: 188 Key: E; e; E   Time Sig.: 2/2; 2/4; 2/2;
    3/2; 2/2 Directive words: m.178 Swell
    Incipit: 5315617654555 Timing: 8:46
Reprints by Billings: None   Reprints by others: **122** 24
Recordings: AS

294. By The Rivers of Watertown

Billings's Title: LAMENTATION OVER BOSTON. An Anthem
Location: Singing Master's Assistant p.33-38
        Complete Works: II, p.136-147
Source of Text: Billings's paraphrase of Psalm 137:1,
    Jeremiah 3:21, 31:20
No. of meas: 133   Key: a   Time Sig.: 3/2 and 2/2
    intermixed   Directive words: None   Incipit:
    1512322213217 Timing: 5:45
Reprints by Billings: None   Reprints by others: None
Notes: Billings's text towards the end of the anthem also
    used for JARGON (**146** 102)
Literature: MacDougall 59
Recordings: I, R, T, U, AK, AU

295. David, The King, Was Grieved

Billings's Title: DAVID'S LAMENTATION
Location: Singing Master's Assistant p.22
        Complete Works: II, p.108
Source of Text: Bible, Authorized Version, II Samuel
    18:33, with alterations by Billings
No. of meas: 30   Key: a   Time Sig.: 2/4

Directive words: None Incipit: 1123232342771
Timing: 0:52
Reprints by Billings: None   Reprints by others: 30 16; **32**
72, 33 72, **36** 168, **38** 142, **39** 142, **83** 97, **90** 61; **91** 58,
141 122, **180** 115
Recordings: A, G, R, S, Y, Z, AA, AB, AK, AR, AS, AT

296. Down Steers The Bass

Billings's Title: CONSONANCE An Anthem.
Location: Psalm-Singer's Amusement, p.81-89
          Complete Works: III, p.113-119
Source of Text: "On Music" by Mather Byles, published in
     NEPS, p.10
No. of meas: 101   Key: C   Time Sig.: 2/2; 3/2; 2/2
     Directive words: None   Incipit: B:1531234551S:512
     Timing: 3:55
Reprints by Billings: None   Reprints by others: **122** 81
Literature: KroegerWP 55,
Recordings: K, R

297. Except The Lord Build The House

Billings's Title: An Anthem   Psalm 127
Location: Independent Publication ca.1786-90
          Complete Works: III, p.236-243
Source of Text: Bible, Psalms, Common Prayer version,
     Psalm 127:1-4, 6, with alterations by Billings
No. of meas: 120   Key: A   Time Sig.: 2/4,6/8, and 2/2
     intermixed; 2/4   Directive words: m.75 "This strain no
     faster than Largo"   Incipit: B:1121517656543
     Timing: 3:57
Reprints by Billings: None   Reprints by others: None
Notes: At foot of p.1: "Set this piece in G."

298. God Is The King

Billings's Title: PEACE, An Anthem. Words from sundry
     Scriptures and elsewhere
Location: Independent Publication (ca.1783)
          Complete Works: III, p.257-275

Source of Text: Bible, Psalms, Common Prayer version,
    Psalm 47:7; Authorized Version, Psalm 97:1, 106:48;
    Deuteronomy 32:43 (paraphrased); Revelation 11:15; Luke
    2:14; Isaiah 11:6-9, 49:23; Isaac Watts, Hymns I,
    No.10, v.1-2; with Billings's additions and
    alterations.
No. of meas: 343   Key: D   Time Sig.: 2/2; 6/4; 3/2; 2/4;
    2/2; 6/4; 3/2; 6/4; 2/4   Directive words: m.108
    Sprightly; m.199 Sprightly   Incipit: 5112176223217
    Timing: 11:47
Reprints by Billings: None   Reprints by others: None
Notes: This is one of only two anthems by Billings which
    include parts designed for instruments. The
    instrumental prelude, postlude, and interludes appear
    to have been intended for a small group of instruments
    rather than for organ. Billings assigned no specific
    instruments to any part, occupying staves otherwise
    assigned to voices when they are not singing.
       The "Hallelujah" section (mm.86-97) appears in a
    slightly revised and expanded form in Billings's
    hymn-tune RESURRECTION (ca.1787), and a slightly
    revised version of mm.310-334 comprises the final
    section of Billings's AN ANTHEM FOR ORDINATION (O Thou
    To Whom)
Literature: Daniel 106

299. Hark! Hark! Hear You Not

Billings's Title: An Anthem for Christmas
Location: Continental Harmony p.117-127
          Complete Works: IV, p.173-186
Source of Text: Bible, Authorized Version, Luke 2:10-14;
    Matthew 21:9; Isaac Watts, Horae Lyricae, "The Nativity
    of Christ", v.7-8; some words probably by Billings.
No. of meas: 209 (210)   Key: C   Time Sig.: 2/2, 3/4, and
    2/4 intermixed; 2/2 and 6/4 intermixed; 3/4   Directive
    words: None   Incipit: 1111132555543 Timing: 7:44
Reprints by Billings: None   Reprints by others: None
Notes: The first 31 m. of the anthem appear as a
    fuging-tune called HADLEY in the CtHT-W Ms and MiU-C
    Ms3 (WBIII, p.322-323), probably dating from the 1770s

or early 1780s. Note at bottom of page: "N.B. Set this
piece one note lower."
<u>Recordings</u>: N

300. Hear, Hear, O Heav'ns

<u>Billings's Title</u>: An Anthem For Fast Day
<u>Location</u>: Continental Harmony p.42-47
           Complete Works: IV, p.47-54
<u>Source of Text</u>: Bible, Authorized Version, Isaiah 1:2-4,
    16, 18; Isaiah 56:1
<u>No. of meas</u>: 123   <u>Key</u>: f   <u>Time Sig</u>.: 2/2; 3/4; 4/4
    <u>Directive words</u>: None <u>Incipit</u>: 5171556765453
      <u>Timing</u>: 5:18
<u>Reprints by Billings</u>: None   <u>Reprints by others</u>: None
<u>Notes</u>: At head of music: "Set this piece in E."
<u>Recordings</u>: R, T

301. Hear My Prayer, O Lord

<u>Billings's Title</u>: An Anthem   Psalm the 143 for Fast Day
<u>Location</u>: New-England Psalm-Singer, p.81-85
           Complete Works: I, p.293-301
<u>Source of Text</u>: Bible, Authorized Version, Psalm
    143:1-2,5-8; with Billings's additions and alterations.
<u>No. of meas</u>: 107 (123) <u>Key</u>: a   <u>Time Sig</u>.: 3/2; 3/4; C
<u>Directive words</u>: m.1 Divoto; m.48 Divoto; m.51
    Lamentatone; m.58 Vigoroso; m.74 Largo; m.101 Adagio
    <u>Incipit</u>: 1354323457654 <u>Timing</u>: 7:18
<u>Reprints by Billings</u>: None   <u>Reprints by others</u>: None

302. Hear My Prayer, O Lord

<u>Billings's Title</u>: An Anthem   Psalm 39th.
<u>Location</u>: Singing Master's Assistant p.26-27
           Complete Works: II, p.118-121
<u>Source of Text</u>: Bible, Authorized Version, Psalm 39:12-13
<u>No. of meas</u>: 42   <u>Key</u>: b   <u>Time Sig</u>.: 3/2; 2/2; 3/4; 6/4
<u>Directive words</u>: None <u>Incipit</u>: 1232321712321
    <u>Timing</u>: 2:06
<u>Reprints by Billings</u>: None   <u>Reprints by others</u>: None

303. I Am Come Into My Garden

Billings's Title: An Anthem   Solomons' Songs, Chap. 5th
Location: Continental Harmony p.76-81
          Complete Works: IV, p.113-119
Source of Text: Bible, Authorized Version, The Song of
    Solomon 5:1-2,6; 2:5; 8:14
No. of meas: 118   Key: a   Time Sig.: 2/2; 2/4; 2/2; 2/4
    Directive words: m.98 Vigoroso   Incipit: 1712345123217
    Timing: 3:12
Reprints by Billings: None   Reprints by others: None
Literature: WienandtAEA 200-1;
Recordings: F, Q

304. I Am The Rose Of Sharon

Billings's Title: An Anthem   Solomon's Songs, Chap. 2d.
Location: Singing Master's Assistant p.73-78
          Complete Works: II, p.216-225
Source of Text: Bible, Authorized Version, The Song of
    Solomon 2:1-5, 7-8, 10-11
No. of meas: 141   Key: A   Time Sig.: 2/4; 6/4; 2/4;
    6/8; 2/4; 6/4   Directive words: None
    Incipit: S:5121231712176 Timing: 3:39
Reprints by Billings: None   Reprints by others: 1 33, 2
    33, 3 33, 4 53, 5 53, 6 53, 32 87, 33 87, 38 132, 39
    132, 82 98, 89 142, 90 153, 145 197, 178 73, 179 73
Literature: KroegerWP 50,
Recordings: L, M, R, AF

305. I Charge You, O Ye Daughters

Billings's Title: An Anthem. Solomon's Songs
Location: Continental Harmony p.155-159
          Complete Works: IV, p.233-238
Source of Text: Bible, Authorized Version, The Song of
    Solomon 2:7, 5:8-12; some alterations by Billings.
No. of meas: 94   Key: C   Time Sig.: 3/4, 2/4, and 6/8
    intermixed   Directive words: None
    Incipit: S:5111232121765 Timing: 2:31
Reprints by Billings: None   Reprints by others: None

306. I Heard A Great Voice

Billings's Title: A Funeral Anthem   Rev. Chap. 14th.
Location: Singing Master's Assistant p.52-53
          Complete Works: II, p.175
Source of Text: Bible, Authorized Version, Revelation
    14:13
No. of meas: 35   Key: f   Time Sig.: 3/2 and 2/2
    intermixed; 4/4   Directive words: m.33 Minim Beating
    Incipit: 1551765543455   Timing: 2:22
Reprints by Billings: None   Reprints by others: 11 88,
    12 88, 13 88, 36 166, 38 130, 39 130, 50 106, 61 77, 62
    108, 64 108, 73 78, 74 126, 84 48, 89 75, 90 76, 92 86,
    93 86, 94 86, 95 86, 96 78, 97 78, 98 78, 99 78, 100
    78, 101 78, 102 83, 126 38, 176 96, 178 86, 179 86
Manuscripts: MHi Ms
Recordings: S

307. I Love The Lord

Billings's Title: GRATITUDE. An Anthem. Psalm 116th.
Location: Singing Master's Assistant p.63-67
          Complete Works: II, p.194-199
Source of Text: Bible, Authorized Version, Psalm 116:1-3;
    Psalm 54:7; II Chronicles 30:9; Exodus 34:6-7; Nehemiah
    9:17; Psalm 89:52; Psalm 106:48
No. of meas: 93   Key: C; c; C   Time Sig.: 3/4; 2/2
    Directive words: m.87 Divoto   Incipit: 5123143231217
    Timing: 3:54
Reprints by Billings: None   Reprints by others: None
Literature: Daniel 239

308. I Will Love Thee

Billings's Title: DELIVERANCE, An Anthem. Words from
    sundry scriptures, &c.
Location: Continental Harmony p.131-137
          Complete Works: IV, p.195-205
Source of Text: Bible, Authorized Version, Psalm 18:1,

6-7, 9, 13, 17, 38, 41; Isaac Watts, Psalm 116, Part
II, v. 1; additional words probably by Billings.
No. of meas: 186   Key: C   Time Sig.: 2/4 and 3/4
   intermixed; 6/4; 2/2; 3/2   Directive words: m.173
   Swell   Incipit: 5511335543212 Timing: 5:20
Reprints by Billings: None   Reprints by others: None
Literature: Daniel 244
Recordings: T

309. Is Any Afflicted

Billings's Title: An Anthem taken from Sundry Scriptures
Location: Singing Master's Assistant p.30-31
            Complete Works: II, p.128-131
Source of Text: Bible, Authorized Version, James 5:13;
   Ephesians 5:19; Colossians 3:16
No. of meas: 45   Key: g; G   Time Sig.: 2/2 and 3/2
   intermixed   Directive words: None   Incipit:
   1123454343211 Timing: 2:07
Reprints by Billings: None   Reprints by others: None
Manuscripts: MHi Ms
Notes: The "Shepard Fish" Ms at MHi has an extra 4
   measures between m.5 and m.6, repeating the previous
   text and ending the phrase on the tonic.

310. Let Ev'ry Mortal Ear Attend

Billings's Title: An Anthem Isaiah 55   suitable to be
   sung at a Communion.
Location: Psalm-Singer's Amusement, p.89-99
            Complete Works: III, p.120-129
Source of Text: Isaac Watts, Hymns I, No.7, v.1; Bible,
   Authorized Version, Isaiah 55:1-2; Revelation 22:17,
   20; with Billings's additions and alterations.
No. of meas: 143   Key: a; A   Time Sig.: 3/2; 2/2 and
   3/2 intermixed; 2/2   Directive words: None
   Incipit: B:1176543232123 Timing: 7:06
Reprints by Billings: None   Reprints by others: 122 89

311. Lift Up Your Eyes

Billings's Title: An Anthem. Word[s] by Dr. Watts.
Location: Suffolk Harmony p.30-33
          Complete Works: III, p.177-179
Source of Text: Isaac Watts, Hymns II, No.43, v.6-7
No. of meas: 41   Key: F; C; F   Time Sig.: 3/4 and 4/4
    intermixed; 6/4 Directive words: m.36 Shout and Swell
    Incipit: 1351553516543 Timing: 1:20
Reprints by Billings: None   Reprints by others: 1 51, 2
    51, 3 51, 4 78, 5 71, 6 71
Literature: KroegerWP 50; WienandtAEA 205

312. Mourn, Mourn

Billings's Title: An Anthem for Fast Day. Some of the
    words from scripture.
Location: Continental Harmony p.145-151
          Complete Works: IV, p.217-225
Source of Text: Joel 2:18-19, 21; most of the words,
    however, seem to be Billings's own
No. of meas: 164   Key: c; C   Time Sig.: 3/2 and 2/2
    intermixed; 2/4; 2/2; 2/4 2/2; 6/4 Directive words:
    None Incipit: 1171555111776 Timing: 6:07
Reprints by Billings: None   Reprints by others: None
Notes: A change of mode from C minor to C major was
    apparently omitted by the typesetters at m.62.
Recordings: F, J, P, V, AO

313. My Friends, I Am Going

Billings's Title: THE DYING CHRISTIAN'S LAST FAREWELL
Location: Continental Harmony p.164-168
          Complete Works: IV, p.245-250
Source of Text: Anonymous, possibly by Billings, but a
    setting of the same text was made by Jacob French,
    published in his New American Melody (Boston, 1789).
No. of meas: 73   Key: g   Time Sig.: 2/2 and 3/2
    intermixed; 2/4, 2/2, and 3/2 intermixed; 4/4
    Directive words: m.57 Affettuoso; m.61 Languishing;

m.71 Affettuoso. Minum Beating   Incipit: 5122334451231
  Timing: 4:13
Reprints by Billings: None   Reprints by others: None
Notes: title followed by the note: "spoken in the Tenor."
Literature: KroegerWP 57; WienandtAEA 200
Recordings: E, AO

314. O Clap Your Hands

Billings's Title: An Anthem. Psalm 47. For
  Thanksgiving.
Location: Independent Publication (ca.1786-1789)
          Complete Works: III, p.252-255
Source of Text: Perez Morton, poem published in NEPS with
  QUEEN STREET (see WBI, p.188-189)
No. of meas: 44   Key: G   Time Sig.: 2/2, 6/4, amd 2/2
  intermixed Directive words: None
  Incipit: 1121232123434 Timing: 1:51
Reprints by Billings: None   Reprints by others: None

315. O God, My Heart Is Fixed

Billings's Title: An Anthem.   Psalm 108. For Thanksgiving
  Day Morning.
Location: Continental Harmony p.176-184
          Complete Works: IV, p.264-273
Source of Text: Bible, Authorized Version, Psalm 108:1, 5,
  12-13; Common Prayer version, Psalm 108:2; some
  alterations and additions by Billings.
No. of meas: 147   Key: G; g; G   Time Sig.: 2/2; 3/2 and
  2/2 intermixed; 2/4; 2/2; 2/4; 3/2   Directive words:
  None   Incipit: 123451543217 Timing: 5:54
Reprints by Billings: None   Reprints by others: None

316. O God, Thou Hast Been Displeased

Billings's Title: VARIETY, WITHOUT METHOD. An Anthem.
  Psalm 60.
Location: Continental Harmony p.138-143
          Complete Works: IV, p.206-213
Source of Text: Bible, Psalms, The Book of Common Prayer

version, Psalm 60:1-2, 4-5, 9-11; Bible, Authorized
Version, Psalm 60:12; some alterations and additions by
Billings.
No. of meas: 150   Key: g; c; C; c; F; f; C; F
    Time Sig.: 2/2 and 3/2 intermixed; 2/4, 3/4, and 4/4
    intermixed; 2/2; 4/4; 2/2 and 3/2 intermixed
    Directive words: m.74 Crotchet Beating; m.147 Swell
    Incipit: 1112323332345 Timing: 5:32
Reprints by Billings: None   Reprints by others: None
Literature: Daniel 113

317. O Praise God

Billings's Title: UNIVERSAL PRAISE: An Anthem, for
    Thanksgiving Day taken from Psalm 149, &c.
Location: Continental Harmony p.97-104
         Complete Works: IV, p.145-155
Source of Text: Bible, Psalms, Common Prayer version,
    Psalm 150:1; the rest of the text apparently is
    Billings's own paraphrase of Psalms 148 and 150.
No. of meas: 177   Key: C   Time Sig.: 2/2; 2/4; 2/2; 6/4
    and 2/2 intermixed; 3/2 Directive words: None
    Incipit: 1713235455432   Timing: 6:47
Reprints by Billings: Ind pub (Boston: Thomas and Andrews,
    1793) Reprints by others: None
Literature: KroegerWP 56; WienandtAEA 203

318. O Praise The Lord Of Heaven

Billings's Title: An Anthem for Thanksgiving. Psalm 148.
Location: Continental Harmony p.35-41
         Complete Works: IV, p.39-46
Source of Text: Bible, Psalms, The Book of Common Prayer
    version, Psalm 148:1-2, 5, 7-8, 10-12; additional text
    from the Earl of Roscommon's version of Psalm 148;
    additions and alterations by Billings.
No. of meas: 106   Key: F   Time Sig.: 3/4 and 4/4
    intermixed; 2/4, 3/4 and 2/2 intermixed; 4/4;
    Directive words: None Incipit: 5567176711A:176
    Timing: 5:27
Reprints by Billings: None   Reprints by others: None

Literature: KroegerWP 57,
Recordings: D, L, Q

319. O Thou To Whom All Creatures Bow

Billings's Title: An Anthem for Ordination. Words from
    Tate and Brady, Scripture, &c.
Location: Continental Harmony p.105-116
            Complete Works: IV, p.157-171
Source of Text: Brady and Tate, Psalm 8, v.1; Bible,
    Authorized Version, Malachi 3:3, Isaiah 35:5, 52:7,
    Luke 2:14; Bible, Psalms, Common Prayer version, Psalm
    132:17, 68:11, 115:1; with additions and alterations by
    Billings.
No. of meas: 239   Key: C; F; C   Time Sig.: 3/2; 4/4;
    3/2; 4/4; 2/4; 4/4 and 3/2 intermixed; 6/4; 4/4; 2/4
    Directive words: None   Incipit: 1175654332531
    Timing: 8:50
Reprints by Billings: None   Reprints by others: None
Notes: Two sections in this anthem were previously printed
    by Billings: mm.144-164 are essentially the same as
    mm.164-181 of RETROSPECT (Was Not The Day), and
    mm.215-239 are substantially the same as the ending of
    PEACE (God Is The King).
    This anthem is one of only two Billings's anthems to
    include an independent instrumental part. The music
    between mm.165-168 and mm.199-202 are interludes for
    unspecified instruments, designed to introduce a change
    of key.
Literature: Daniel 106

320. Praise The Lord, O My Soul

Billings's Title: An Anthem. Ps 103
Location: New York Public Library Ms
            Complete Works: III, p.336-339
Source of Text: Bible, Psalms, Common Prayer version,
    Psalm 103:1-3; with additions and alterations by
    Billings.
No. of meas: 59 (73) Key: C   Time Sig.: 3/2; 3/4; C
    Directive words: None   Incipit: 1512345432123

Timing: 5:32
Reprints by Billings: None   Reprints by others: None
Notes: two copies of the anthem are in the NN Ms.

321. Samuel The Priest

Billings's Title: FUNERAL ANTHEM. Words from Sundry
Scriptures.
Location: Suffolk Harmony p.52-56
           Complete Works: III, p.214-219
Source of Text: Bible, Authorized Version, I Samuel 25:1
    (paraphrased), Job 1:21, 19:21; Psalm 88:18, 6:6,
    119:25, 28; with alterations by Billings.
No. of meas: 101   Key: a   Time Sig.: 4/4
    Directive words: None Incipit: 1123234543253
    Timing: 5:39
Reprints by Billings: None   Reprints by others: 54 149(v)
Manuscripts: MHi Ms
Notes: The MHi Ms is entitled "An Anthem Words from Job".
    It is in G minor and begins with the text "Have pity on
    me." This version probably predates the published
    version, which was sung at the funeral of Rev. Samuel
    Cooper on 2 January 1784. The Ms version, transposed
    to A minor, was published by Jacob French in 54
Literature: AndersonFSC

322. Sanctify A Fast

Billings's Title: An Anthem. Joel 1st and 2d Chap.
    Suitable for Fast.
Location: Continental Harmony p.186-197
           Complete Works: IV, p.278-291
Source of Text: Bible, Authorized Version, Joel 1:14,
    17-20; 2:15, 17, 21, 23-24, 26, 32; with alterations
    and additions by Billings.
No. of meas: 241   Key: g; G   Time Sig.: 2/2 and 3/2
    intermixed; 2/4; 2/2   Directive words: None
    Incipit: 1234512321711 Timing: 8:17
Reprints by Billings: None   Reprints by others: None

323. Sing Praises To The Lord

Billings's Title: An Anthem. For Thanksgiving Day
    Morning.
Location: Continental Harmony p.70-74
         Complete Works: IV, p.103-108
Source of Text: A composite of lines from Psalm 30:4-5
    from both the Bible, Authorized Version, and Common
    Prayer version, probably by Billings.
No. of meas: 92   Key: C   Time Sig.: 3/2 and 2/2
    intermixed   Directive words: None
    Incipit: 5111333121543 Timing: 5:09
Reprints by Billings: None   Reprints by others: None

324. Sing Ye Merrily

Billings's Title: An Anthem. Psalm 81st.
Location: Singing Master's Assistant p.57-62
         Complete Works: II, p.184-191
Source of Text: Bible, Psalms, Book of Common Prayer
    version, Psalm 81:1-4; the Lesser Doxology.
No. of meas: 124   Key: C   Time Sig.: 2/2; 3/4 and 2/4
    intermixed; 2/2; 2/4; 2/2 Directive words: None
    Incipit: 1511132333545 Timing: 4:39
Reprints by Billings: None   Reprints by others : None
Literature: KroegerWP 51,

325. The Beauty of Israel

Billings's Title: An Anthem. 2d Samuel Chap. 1st.
Location: Psalm-Singer's Amusement, p.16-21
         Complete Works: III, p.24-31
Source of Text: Bible, Authorized Version, II Samuel
    1:19-20, 23-24, 26-27; with additions and alterations
    by Billings.
No. of meas: 143   Key: f; F; f   Time Sig.: 2/2; 2/4;
    2/2; 4/4   Directive words: None
    Incipit: 1543654322345 Timing: 4:51
Reprints by Billings: None   Reprints by others: 119 16

326. The Heavens Declare

Billings's Title: SUBLIMITY. An Anthem. Psalm 19. This
   subject is both Praise and Prayer, it may answer for
   Thanksgiving or Fast.
Location: Continental Harmony p.171-176
          Complete Works: IV, p.257-263
Source of Text: Bible, Psalms, Common Prayer version,
   Psalm 19:1-2, 4, 8, 14; Authorized Version, Psalm 19:3;
   with additions and alterations by Billings.
No. of meas: 100   Key: C   Time Sig.: 2/2; 2/4 and 2/2
   intermixed; 2/4; 2/2; C   Directive words: None
   Incipit: 5117171217656 Timing: 5:09
Reprints by Billings: None   Reprints by others: None

327. The Lord Descended From Above

Billings's Title: An Anthem. Psalm 18
Location: New-England Psalm-Singer, p.51-56
          Complete Works: I, p.191-201
Source of Text: Sternhold and Hopkins, The Booke of
   Psalms, Psalm 18:9-10; with additions by Billings.
No. of meas: 136 (150)   Key: C   Time Sig.: 3/4; 2/2;
   3/4; 2/2; 3/2; 3/4; 2/2; 3/2; C Directive words: m.1
   Vigoroso; m.35 Grave; m.99 Choro Grando; m.132 Adagio.
   Incipit: 1156712176551 Timing: 8:19
Reprints by Billings: None   Reprints by others: None

328. The Lord Is King

Billings's Title: An Anthem. Psalm 93
Location: New-England Psalm-Singer, p.24-30
          Complete Works: I, p.124-135
Source of Text: Bible, Authorized Version, Psalm 93; with
   additions and alterations by Billings.
No. of meas: 150 (155)   Key: C   Time Sig.: 3/4; 3/2;
   2/4; 3/2; 3/4; 3/2; C Directive words: m.74 Divoto;
   m.101 Maestuso; m.114 Divoto; m.123 Vigoroso; m.138
   Adagio (Divoto);   Incipit: 1121765511123
   Timing: 9:53
Reprints by Billings: None   Reprints by others: None

329. The Lord Is Ris'n Indeed

Bi'lings's Title: An Anthem for Easter. Words from
    Scripture & Dr. Young.
Location: Independent Publication (1787)
            Complete Works: III, p.245-251
Source of Text: Bible, Authorized Version, Luke 24:34;
    I Corinthians 15:20; Edward Young, The Complaint, or
    Night Thoughts, Night the Fourth, lines 271-273,
    288-293, 298-300.
No. of meas: 101 without addition; 125 with addition
    Key: A   Time Sig.: 2/4   Directive words: None
    Incipit: B:156751712321T:5 Timing: 2:27 without
    addition; 2:51 with addition
Reprints by Billings: Ind pub (1795)   Reprints by others:
    11 90, 12 90, 13 90, 21 134, 25 34, 32 84, 33 84, 38
    114, 39 114, 41 49(v), 48 116, 49 86, 50 101, 54
    133(exp), 64 107, 65 81, 74 121(exp), 83 87, 89 70, 96
    89, 97 89, 98 89, 99 89, 100 89, 101 89, 102 94, 104
    81, 105 101(exp), 107 138, 108 138, 110 60(v), 125 5,
    129 97, 130 97, 134 106(v), 135 174, 138 40, 143 55,
    148 1, 152 170, 153 170(exp), 154 170, 155 209, 156
    204, 157 204, 158 204, 159 272, 170 95, 171 80, 172
    130, 173 90, 178 88, 179 88
Notes: Billings's reprint of 1795 includes an added
    24-measure section between mm.65 and 66 of the 1787
    version. The new text also comes from Young's The
    Complaint. No copy of Billings's original print of the
    expanded version survives; however, it was reprinted by
    others at least five times. The abbreviation "exp" in
    the reprint list above indicates the expanded version.
Literature: CrawfordCR xxiv; KroegerWBEA
Recordings: A, O, R, S, AC

330. The States, O Lord

Billings's Title: INDEPENDENCE
Location: Singing Master's Assistant p.91-99
            Complete Works: II, p.244-255
Source of Text: Isaac Watts, Psalm 21:1 (paraphrased);

Brady and Tate, Psalm 21:3 (paraphrased); other text
probably by Billings.
No. of meas: 175   Key: D   Time Sig.: 2/2; 2/4; 2/2;
2/4; 3/2   Directive words: m.171 Slow
Incipit: 5565512123434 Timing: 7:32
Reprints by Billings: None   Reprints by others: None
Recordings: AU

331. They That Go Down To The Sea

Billings's Title: EUROCLYDON, An Anthem. Psalms [sic] 107
for Mariners.
Location: Psalm-Singer's Amusement, p.54-60
         Complete Works: III, p.71-79
Source of Text: Bible, Psalms, The Book of Common Prayer
version, Psalm 107:23-24; Authorized Version, Psalm
107:25-30; with alterations and additions by Billings.
No. of meas: 156   Key: f-sharp; F-sharp   Time Sig.:
2/2; 2/4   Directive words: m.147 Vigoroso
Incipit: B:171T:5321543456 Timing: 4:28
Reprints by Billings: None   Reprints by others: **122** 54,
145 181
Literature: KroegerWP 52,

332. Thou, O God, Art Praised

Billings's Title: An Anthem
Location: Psalm-Singer's Amusement, p.9-16
         Complete Works: III, p.17-23
Source of Text: Bible, Psalms, The Book of Common Prayer
version, Psalm 65:1-2, 12-14; with alterations and
additions by Billings.
No. of meas: 125   Key: C   Time Sig.: 2/2; 2/4; 2/2; 3/2
Directive words: m.115 Allegro   Incipit: 1512343454322
Timing: 3:36
Reprints by Billings: None   Reprints by others: **122** 9
Literature: KroegerWP 52,

333. Vital Spark Of Heav'nly Flame

Billings's Title: THE DYING CHRISTIAN TO HIS SOUL.   An

Anthem. Words by Pope.
Location: Psalm-Singer's Amusement, p.99-102
          Complete Works: III, p.130-133
Source of Text: Alexander Pope, "The Dying Christian to
   his Soul", An Ode, in Pope, Works (London: Knapton,
   1751), v.5, p.190.
No. of meas: 68   Key: b; B   Time Sig.: 2/2, 2/4 and 3/2
   intermixed; 2/2; 6/8; 2/4; 2/2   Directive words: m.35
   Languissiant;   Incipit: 15123217B:51765   Timing: 2:15
Reprints by Billings: None   Reprints by others: 25 52, 81
   9, 82 41, 84 44, 122 99, 145 206, 175 83
Literature: KroegerWP 54,

334. Was Not The Day Dark And Gloomy

Billings's Title: RETROSPECT, An Anthem from Sundry
   Scriptures
Location: Singing Master's Assistant p.81-90
          Complete Works: II, p.231-243
Source of Text: Bible, Authorized Version, paraphrases of
   Psalm 124:7, Jeremiah 48:10, 4:19, 47:6; Psalm 51:8;
   Isaiah 2:4, 52:7, Luke 2:14; Revelation 19:6, all
   probably by Billings
No. of meas: 196   Key: a; A; a; A   Time Sig.: 2/2; 3/2
   and 2/2 intermixed; 2/4; 2/2 and 3/2 intermixed; 3/2,
   2/2 and 3/4 intermixed   Directive words: m.50
   Affetuoso; m.181 Maistuso Choro Grando   Incipit:
   1171554554321 Timing: 7:13
Reprints by Billings: None   Reprints by others: None
Notes: Mm.100-109 appear as the hymn-tune GOSPEL POOL in
   75 121; mm.163-180 appear in Billings's Ordination
   Anthem, O Thou To Whom All Creatures Bow
Recordings: T, AT

335. We Are Met For A Concert

Billings's Title: MODERN MUSIC
Location: Psalm-Singer's Amusement, p.72-77
          Complete Works: III, p.97-103
Source of Text: Probably by Billings
No. of meas: 94   Key: E; e; E   Time Sig.: 2/2; 2/4;

2/2; 2/4; 3/2; 6/4   Directive words: None
Incipit: 1233451765434 Timing: 3:01
Reprints by Billings: None   Reprints by others: **122** 72
Notes: At head of music Billings has added these
   directions: "N.B. after the audience are seated & the
   Performers have taken the pitch slyly from the leader
   the Song begins."
Literature: KroegerWP 55,
Recordings: Q, R, Y

336. We Have Heard With Our Ears

Billings's Title: An Anthem. Psalm 44th. Suitable to be
   Sung on the Anniversary of our Fore-father's Landing,
   and for Thanksgiving.
Location: Continental Harmony p.84-94
         Complete Works: IV, p.127-140
Source of Text: Bible, Authorized Version, Psalm 44:1-4,
   23, 11:2, 32:5 (paraphrased); I Kings 8:30; Psalm 45:3;
   Exodus 15:9-10, 18 (paraphrased); Psalm 106:48; some
   text probably by Billings.
No. of meas: 242 (241)   Key: E; e; E   Time Sig.: 2/2;
   3/2; 2/2; 3/2 and 2/2 intermixed; 3/4; 2/2; 3/2; 2/2;
   3/2 Directive words: m.138 Vigoroso; m.189 Fortissimo
   Incipit: 1233456715432 Timing: 10:38
Reprints by Billings: None   Reprints by others: None

337. When The Lord Turn'd Again

Billings's Title: An Anthem. Psalm 126
Location: Continental Harmony 160-164
         Complete Works: IV, p.239-244
Source of Text: A composite from Bible, Psalms, Common
   Prayer version, Psalm 126:1-6, and Authorized Version,
   Psalm 126:1-5; with additions and alterations by
   Billings.
No. of meas: 93   Key: F   Time Sig.: 2/2
   Directive words: None   Incipit: 1232343454323
   Timing: 4:50
Reprints by Billings: None   Reprints by others: None

338. Who Is This That Cometh From Edom

Billings's Title: An Anthem Taken from sundry Scriptures
Location: Psalm-Singer's Amusement, p.63-71
        Complete Works: III, p.84-95
Source of Text: Bible, Authorized Version, Isaiah 63:1,
    9:6; Genesis 49:10; Isaiah 7:14; Revelation 1:11;
    Matthew 1:23; Jeremiah 23:6; Genesis 3:15; John 1:29,
    5:18, John 1:17; Psalm 85:10, 107:8; Isaac Watts, Hymns
    I, no.58, v.4; with additional text probably by
    Billings.
No. of meas: 188   Key: E; e; E   Time Sig.: 2/2; 2/4;
    3/2 and 2/2 intermixed; 4/4; 6/4; 4/4   Directive
    words: m.140 Beat Crotchets; m.141 Vigoroso; m.178
    Minum Beating   Incipit: 5551717656715   Timing: 7:20
Reprints by Billings: None   Reprints by others: 54 140,
    122 63

List of Works Cited

Abbreviations and Short Titles
Used in the Catalog

I. American Tunebooks

1. AdgatePH   Adgate, Andrew, and Ishmael Spicer. The
Philadelphia Harmony. Philadelphia:
M'Culloch, 1789.   [E21629]

2. AdgatePH(1790)   Adgate, Andrew, and Ishmael Spicer. The
Philadelphia Harmony. Philadelphia:
Westcott and Adgate, [1790]. [E22299]

3. AdgatePH(1791)   Adgate, Andrew, and Ishmael Spicer.
The Philadelphia Harmony. Philadelphia:
the Authors,[1791]. [E46100]

4. AdgatePH(1796)   Adgate, Andrew. The Philadelphia
Harmony, Philadelphia: Carey, 1796.
[E29953]

5. AdgatePH(1801)   Adgate, Andrew. The Philadelphia
Harmony, [7th ed.] Philadelphia:
Carey, 1801. [S22]

6. AdgatePH(1807)   Adgate, Andrew. The Philadephia
Harmony, [9th ed.] Philadelphia:
Carey, 1807. [S11948]

7. AlbeeNC   Albee, Amos. The Norfolk Collection of
Sacred Harmony. Dedham: H. Mann, 1805.
[S7845]

8. AllenNYS   Allen, Francis D. The New York Selection
                     of Sacred Music. New York: M'Dermut,
                     1818. [S43050]

9. Am Mus Mag   The American Musical Magazine, v.1, no.1
                     (Oct.1800), no.2 (Jan.1801), no.3
                     (Apr.1801), no.4 (July 1801).
                     Northampton: Andrew Wright.

10. ArmstrongPS   Armstrong, John. The Pittsburgh
                     Selection of Psalm Tunes. Pittsburgh:
                     Cramer, Spear, & Eichbaum, 1816.

11. AtwillNYC   Atwill, Thomas H. The New York
                     Collection of Sacred Harmony.
                     Lansingburgh: [n.p.], 1795. [E28216]

12. AtwillNYC2   Atwill, Thomas H. The New York
                     Collection of Sacred Harmony. [Walpole,
                     NH: Thomas and Thomas], 1802. [S1786]

13. AtwillNYVC   Atwill, Thomas H. The New York and
                     Vermont Collection. Albany: Backus and
                     Whiting, 1804. [S7894]

14. BayleyEH2   Bayley, Daniel. The Essex Harmony, or
                     Musical Micellany. Newburyport: Bayley
                     and Son, 1785. [E11560]

15. BayleyNHZ   Bayley, Daniel. New Harmony of Zion.
                     New-buryport: Daniel Bayley, 1788.
                     [E20956]

16. BayleySH   Bayley, Daniel. Select Harmony.
                     Newburyport: Daniel Bayley, [1784].
                     [E18553]

17. BelknapEH   Belknap, Daniel. The Evangelical
                     Harmony. Boston: Thomas and Andrews,
                     1800. [E18925]

18. BelknapMC   Belknap, Daniel, Jr. The Middlesex
                     Collection. Boston: Thomas and Andrews,
                     1802. [S1857]

19. BelknapVC   Belknap, Daniel. The Village
                     Compilation. Boston: J.T. Buckingam,
                     1806. [S9953]

20. BillingsRH   Billings, Nathaniel. The Republican
                     Harmony. Lansingburgh: Silvester
                     Tiffany, 1795.

21. BlakeVH   Blake, George E. _Vocal Harmony_. Phila-
                     delphia: Blake, [ca.1810]. [S8041]

22. Boston Col   _The Boston Collection_. Boston: William
                     Norman, [ca.1799] [E48377]

23. BrownCEH   Brown, Bartholomew, _et al_. _Columbian
                     and European Harmony_. Boston: Thomas
                     and Andrews, 1802. [S1951]

24. BrownCEH2   Brown, Bartholomew, _et al_. _Columbian
                     and European Harmony_, 2d ed. Boston:
                     Thomas and Andrews, 1804. [S5914]

25. BrownsonNC   Brownson, Oliver. _A New Collection of
                     Sacred Harmony_. Simsbury, CT: the
                     Author, 1797. [E31884]

26. BrownsonSH   Brownson, Oliver. _Select Harmony_.
                     [Connecticut: n.p., 1783]. [E17857]

27. BrownsonSH2   Brownson, Oliver. _Select Harmony_.
                     [Connecticut: n.p., ca.1785].

28. BrownsonSH3   Brownson, Oliver. _Select Harmony_.
                     [Connecticut: n.p., ca.1791]. [E23227]

29. BurgerA   Burger, John, Jr., and Cornelium Tibout.
                     Amphion. New York: Burger and Tiebout,
                     [ca.1789].

30. BushnellMS   Bushnell, John. _The Musical Synopsis_.
                     Northampton: Graves and Clap, 1807.
                     [S12255]

31. CH   Billings, William. _The Continental
                     Harmony_. Boston: Thomas and Andrews,
                     1794. [E26673]

32. ChapinMI   Chapin, Nathan, and Joseph L. Dickerson.
                     The Musical Instructor. Philadelphia:
                     W. M'Culloch, 1808. [S14673]

33. ChapinMI2   Chapin, Nathan, and Joseph
                     L. Dickerson. _The Musical Instructer_.
                     Philadelphia: W. M'Culloch, 1810.
                     [S19757]

34 ChildSM   Child, Ebenezer. _The Sacred Musician_.
                     Boston: Maning and Loring, 1804.
                     [S6011]

35. ColeBP2   Cole, John. _The Beauties of Psalmody_,
                     2d ed. Baltimore: Cole and Hewes, 1805.
                     [S8206]

36. CooperBCM   Cooper, William. _The Beauties of Church Music_. Boston: Manning and Loring 1804. [S6079]

37. Cumb Mel   _The Cumberland Melodist_. Philadelphia: William M'Culloch, 1804.

38. DavissonKH2   Davisson, Ananias. _Kentucky Harmony_, 2d ed. Harrisonburg: the Author, [1818] [S37404]

39. DavissonKH5   Davisson, Ananias. _Kentucky Harmony_, 5th ed. Harrisonburg: the Author, 1816. [S43817]

40. DavHarp   _David's Harp_. Baltimore: Neal, Wills, and Cole, 1813. [S43812]

41. DollLU Pt.2   Doll, Joseph. _Leichter Unterricht in der Vocal Musik_, Zweyter Band. Harrisburg: Johann Wyeth, 1815. [S34588]

42. EdsonSH2   Edson, Lewis, Jr. _The Social Harmonist_, 2d ed. New York: [n.p.], 1801. [S433]

43. EdsonSH3   Edson, Lewis, Jr. _The Social Harmonist_, 3d ed. New York: Sage & Clough, 1803. [S4134]

44. ElyBC   Ely, Alexander. _The Baltimore Collection of Church Music_. Baltimore: John Hagerty, 1792.

45. ErbanSM   Erban, Peter. _Sacred Music_. New York: [n.p.], 1808.

46. FH   _The Federal Harmony_. Boston: John Norman, [1788]. [E21485]

47. FH(1790)   _The Federal Harmony_. Boston: John Norman, 1790. [E22919]

48. FH(1792)   _The Federal Harmony_. Boston: John Norman, [ca.1792] [E24831]

49. FH(1794)   _The Federal Harmony_, 8th ed. Boston: William Norman, 1794. [E27762]

50. First Ch C2   _The First Church Collection of Sacred Musick_, 2d ed. Boston: Thomas and Andrew, 1806.

51. FlintCH   Flint, Timothy. _The Columbian Harmonist_. Cincinnati: Looker, Palmer, and Reynolds, 1816. [S37620]

52. FobesDH   Fobes, Azariah. The Delaware Harmony.
                   Philadelphia: W. M'Culloch, 1809.
                   [S17517]

53. FobesDH2   Fobes, Azariah. The Delaware Harmony.
                   Philadelphia: 1814. [S31493]

54. FrenchHOH   French, Jacob. Harmony of Harmony.
                   Northampton: Andrew Wright, 1802.
                   [S2277]

55. FrenchPC   French, Jacob. The Psalmodist's
                   Companion. Worcester: Leonard Worcester,
                   1793. [E25513]

56. GraupnerM   [Graupner, G.] The Monitor, or Celestial
                   Melody. Boston: G. Graupner [1806].
                   [S29186]

57. GilletMS   Gillet, Wheeler. The Maryland
                   Selection. Baltimore: Henry S.
                   Keatinge, 1809. [S18006]

58. GriswoldCH   Griswold, Elijah, and Thomas Skinner.
                   The Connecticut Harmony. [n.p.,
                   ca.1798] [E30521]

59. GriswoldHC   Griswold, Elijah, Stephen Jenks, and
                   John Frisbee. The Hartford Collection.
                   Hartford: Lincoln and Gleason, 1807.
                   [S12689]

60. HartwellCC   Hartwell, Edward. The Chorister's
                   Companion. Exeter: C. Norris & Co.,
                   1815. [S34877]

61. HillVH   Hill, Uri K. The Vermont Harmony,
                   Vol.1. Northampton: Andrew Wright,
                   1801. [S653]

62. HoldenMC   [Holden, Oliver] The Modern Collection
                   of Sacred Music. Boston: Thomas and
                   Andrews, 1800. [E37980]

63. HoldenSS   [Holden, Oliver]. The Suffolk Selection
                   of Church Musick. Boston: Thomas and
                   Andrews, 1807. [S13659]

64. HoldenUH   Holden, Oliver. The Union Harmony, 2
                   vols. Boston: Thomas and Andrews, 1793.
                   [E25619]

65. HoldenUH2   Holden, Oliver. The Union Harmony, 2d
                     ed. Boston: Thomas and Andrews, 1796.
                     [E30573]

66. HoldenUH3   Holden, Oliver. The Union Harmony, 3d
                     ed. Boston: Thomas and Andrews, 1801.
                     [S662]

67. HolyokeCH   Holyoke, Samuel. The Christian
                     Harmonist. Salem: Joshua Cushing, 1804.
                     [S6492]

68. HolyokeCR   Holyoke, Samuel. The Columbian
                     Repository of Sacred Music. Exeter:
                     Henry Ranlet, [1803]. [S2421]

69. HolyokeVC   Holyoke, Samuel. The Vocal Companion.
                     Exeter: Norris and Sawyer, 1807.
                     [S12776]

70. HoweFEE   [Howe, Solomon]. The Farmer's Evening
                     Entertainment. [Northampton: Andrew
                     Wright, 1804] [S6508]

71. HoweWA   [Howe, Solomon]. Worshipper's Assistant.
                     [Northampton: Andrew Wright, ca.1799]

72. HoweYMIC   [Howe, Solomon]. The Young Man's
                     Instructive Companion. Northampton:
                     Andrew Wright, [ca.1804]. [S6512]

73. HuntingtonAC   Huntington, Jonathan. The Albany
                     Collection of Sacred Harmony.
                     Northampton: Andrew Wright, 1800.
                     [S37667]

74. HuntingtonAH   Huntington, Jonathan. The Apollo
                     Harmony. Northampton: Horace Graves,
                     1807. [S12796]

75. IngallsCH   Ingalls, Jeremiah. The Christian
                     Harmony. Exeter: Henry Ranlet, 1805.
                     [S8680]

76. JanesHM   Janes, Walter. The Harmonic Minstrelsy.
                     Dedham: H. Mann, 1807. [S12824]

77. JenksACSM   Jenks, Stephen. The American Compiler
                     of Sacred Music. Northampton: for the
                     Author, 1803. [S4449]

78. JenksCH   Jenks, Stephen. The Christian Harmony.
                     Dedham: Herman Mann, 1811. [S23113]

79. JenksHZ   Jenks, Stephen. _The Harmony of Zion_.
                     Dedham: Daniel Mann, 1818. [S44463]
80. JocelinCC   [Jocelin, Simeon]. _The Chorister's
                     Companion_. New Haven: Simeon Jocelin
                     and Amos Doolittle, 1782. [E17567]
81. JocelinCC Pt3   [Jocelin, Simeon]. _The Chorister's
                     Companion, Part Third_. New Haven: T.
                     and S. Green, [1783]. [E17988]
82. JocelinCC2   [Jocelin, Simeon]. _The Chorister's
                     Companion_, 2d ed. New Haven: Simeon
                     Jocelin, 1788. [E21177]
83. JohnsonTH   Johnson, Alexander. _The Tennessee
                     Harmony_. Cincinnati: Morgan, Lodge &
                     Co., 1818. [S44469]
84. LangdonBP   [Langdon, Chauncey]. _The Beauties of
                     Psalmody_. [New Haven, 1786]. [E19749]
85. LawAS(1800)   Law, Andrew. _The Art of Singing_, 2d ed.
                     [Cheshire: Samuel Andrews], 1800
                     [E37787]
86. LawRM2   Law, Andrew. _The Rudiments of Music_.
                     [Cheshire: William Law, 1786]. [E19057]
87. LawSH   Law, Andrew. _Select Harmony_.
                     Farmington, CT: [William Law, 1779].
                     [E16318]
88. LeslieCH   Leslie, Benjamin. _The Concert Harmony_.
                     Salem: [n.p.], 1811. [S23208]
89. LewisBH   Lewis, Freeman. _The Beauties of
                     Harmony_. Pittsburgh: Cramer, Spear, &
                     Eichbaum, and Freeman Lewis, 1814.
                     [S31923]
90. LewisBH(1818)   Lewis, Freeman. _The Beauties of
                     Harmony_. Pittsburgh: Cramer & Spear, &
                     Eichbaum, 1818 [S44572]
91. LittleEI   Little, William, and William Smith. _The
                     Easy Instructor_. [New York: n.p.,
                     1801]. [S2544]
92. LittleEI(1805)   Little, William, and William Smith. _The
                     Easy Instructor_. Albany: Websters,
                     Skinner, and Steele, 1805. [S8794]

93. LittleEI(1806)   Little, William, and William Smith. The Easy Instructor. Albany: Websters, Skinner, and Steele, 1806. [S10741]

94. LittleEI(1807)   Little, William, and William Smith. The Easy Instructor. Albany: Websters, Skinner, and Steele, 1807. [S12933]

95. LittleEI(1808)   Little, William, and William Smith. The Easy Instructor. Albany: Websters, Skinner, and Steele, 1808. [S15437]

96. LittleEI(1810)   Little, William, and William Smith. The Easy Instructor. Albany: Websters, Skinner, and Steele, [1810?] [S20575]

97. LittleEI(1811)   Little, William, and William Smith. The Easy Instructor. Albany: Websters, Skinner, and Steele, [1811?] [S23233]

98. LittleEI(1812)   Little, William, and William Smith. The Easy Instructor. Albany: Websters, Skinner, and Steele, [1812] [S25869]

99. LittleEI(1813)   Little, William, and William Smith. The Easy Instructor. Albany: Websters, Skinner, and Steele, [1813?] [S28960]

100. LittleEI(1814) Little, William, and William Smith. The Easy Instructor. Albany: Websters, Skinner, and Steele, [1814?] [S31941]

101. LittleEI(1817) Little, William, and William Smith. The Easy Instructor. Albany: Websters, Skinner, and Steele, [1817] [S41275]

102. LittleEI(1818) Little, William, and William Smith. The Easy Instructor. Albany: Websters, Skinner, and Steele, [1818] [S44593]

103. MannMC   Mann, Elias. The Massachusetts Collection. Boston: Manning and Loring, 1807. [S12981]

104. MannNC   Mann, Elias. The Northampton Collection of Sacred Harmony. Northmpton: Andrew Wright, 1797. [E32416]

105. MannNC2   Mann, Elias. The Northampton Collection, [2d ed.]. Northampton: Andrew Wright, 1802. [S2582]

106. Mass Har   The Massachusetts Harmony. Boston: John Norman, [1784]. [E18366]

107. MaximNH   Maxim, Abraham. The Northern Harmony.
                      Exeter: Henry Ranlet, 1805. [S8882]
108. MaximNH2   Maxim, Abraham. The Northern Harmony,
                      2d ed. Exeter: Norris and Sawyer, 1808.
                      [S15586]
109. MaximNH5   Maxim, Abraham. The Northern Harmony,
                      5th ed. Hallowell, ME: E. Goodale,
                      1819.
110. MerrillPBC   Merrill, David. The Psalmodist's Best
                      Companion. Exeter: Henry Ranlet, 1799.
111. MIM   Billings, William. Music in Miniature.
                      Boston: the Author, 1779. [E16205]
112. NEPS   Billings, William. The New-England
                      Psalm-Singer. Boston: Edes and Gill,
                      [1770]. [11572]
113. NeviusNBC   Nevius, John, Cornelius van Deventer,
                      and John Frazee. The New-Brunswick
                      Collection, 2d ed. New Brunswick:
                      William Myer, 1818. [S44974]
114. New Col   A New Collection of Psalm Tunes.
                      [Boston: n.p., ca. 1784]. [E18930]
115. New Eng Har   The New England Harmony. Boston: John
                      Fleeming, 1771.
116. NJ Har   New Jersey Harmony. Philadelphia: John
                      M'Culloch, 1797. [E32547]
117. PattersonCM   Patterson's Church Music. Cincinnati:
                      Brown and Looker, [1813]. [S35573]
118. PattersonCM2   Patterson's Church Music, 2d
                      ed. Cincinnati: Looker and Wallace,
                      1815. [S40474]
119. PilsburyUSSH   Pilsbury, Amos. The United States
                      Sacred Harmony. Boston: Thomas and
                      Andrews, 1799. [E36119]
120. PoolAEH   Pool, David, and Josiah Holbrook.
                      American and European Harmony. Dedham:
                      Herman Mann & Co., 1813. [S29540]
121. PSA   Billings, William. The Psalm-Singer's
                      Amusement. Boston: the Author, 1781.
                      [E17104]
122. PSA post. ed.   Billings, William. The Psalm-Singer's
                      Amusement. [n.p., ca.1804].

123. ReadAMM   Read, Daniel, and Amos Doolittle. The
                    American Musical Magazine, 1 vol. New
                    Haven: the Authors, [1786-7].

124. ReadASB sup.   Read, Daniel. The American Singing
                    Book, 5th ed., supplement. New Haven:
                    the Author, [1796]. [E20673]

125. ReadCH No.2   Read, Daniel. The Columbian Harmonist
                    No.2. New Haven: the Author [1794].
                    [E29390]

126. ReadCH No.3   Read, Daniel. The Columbian Harmonist
                    No.III. New Haven: the Author, [1795]
                    [E29391]

127. ReadCH2   Read, Daniel. The Columbian Harmonist,
                    2d ed. Dedham: Herman Mann, 1804.
                    [S7155]

128. ReadCH3(1806) Read, Daniel. The Columbian Harmonist,
                    3d ed. Dedham: Herman Mann, 1806.
                    [S11251]

129. ReadCH3(1807) Read, Daniel. The Columbian Harmonist,
                    3d ed. Boston: Manning & Loring, 1807.
                    [S13464]

130. ReadCH4   Read, Daniel. The Columbian Harmonist,
                    4th ed. Boston: Manning & Loring, 1810.
                    [S21176]

131. ReadNES   Read, Joel. The New-England Selection.
                    Boston: J.T. Buckingham, 1808. [S16036]

132. ReadNES2   Read, Joel. The New-England Selection,
                    2d ed. Boston: Manning & Loring, 1812.
                    [S26568]

133. ReadNHC   [Read, Daniel, and Simeon Jocelin]. The
                    New Haven Collection of Sacred Music.
                    Dedham: Daniel Mann, 1818. [S44999]

134. ReedMM   Reed, Ephraim. Musical Monitor.
                    Utica: William Williams, 1817. [S41936]

135. RobbinsCH   Robbins, Charles. The Columbian
                    Harmony. Exeter: Henry Ranlet, 1805.

136. Sac Har(1788) Sacred Harmony. Boston: C. Cambridge,
                    [1786-88]. [E22615]

137. Sac Har(1806) Sacred Harmony. Philadelphia: John
                    M'Culloch, 1806. [S11314]

138. SandfordCH   Sandford, E., and J. Rhea. Columbian Harmony. Baltimore: [1793]

139. SangerMH   Sanger, Zedekiah. The Meridian Harmony. Dedham: Herman Mann, 1808. [S16139]

140. Sel Sac Har   A Selection of Sacred Harmony. Philadelphia: W. Young, 1788. [E45213]

141. Sel Sac Har3   A Selection of Sacred Harmony, 3d ed. Philadelphia: W. Young, 1790. [E22884]

142. SeymourMI   Seymour, Lewis, and Thaddeus Seymour. The Musical Instructor. New York: John C. Totten, 1803. [S5038]

143. SeymourNYS2   Seymour, Lewis, and Thaddeus Seymour. The New York Selection of Sacred Music, 2d ed. New York: [n.p.], 1816. [S38917]

144. SH   Billings, William. The Suffolk Harmony. Boston: John Norman, 1786. [E19512]

145. ShumwayAH   Shumway, Nehemiah. The American Harmony. Philadelphia: John M'Culloch, 1793. [E26162]

146. SMA   Billings, William. The Singing Master's Assistant. Boston: Draper and Folsom, 1778. [E15744]

147. SmithEI Pt.2   Smith, William. The Easy Instructor, Part II. [n.p., 1806]. [S11387]

148. StammersPC   Stammers, Edward. The Philadelphia Chorister. Philadelphia: John M'Culloch, 1803. [S5093]

149. StickneyGLMC   Stickney, John. The Gentleman and Lady's Musical Companion. Newburyport: Daniel Bayley, 1774. [E13642]

150. VH1   The Village Harmony. Exeter: Henry Ranlet, 1795.

151. VH2   The Village Harmony, 2d ed. Exeter: Henry Ranlet, 1796. [E31494]

152. VH4   The Village Harmony, 4th ed. Exeter: Henry Ranlet, 1798. [E34930]

153. VH5   The Village Harmony, 5th ed. Exeter: Henry Ranlet, 1800. [E38938]

154. VH6   The Village Harmony, 6th ed. Exeter: Henry Ranlet, 1803. [S5506]

155. VH7   The Village Harmony, 7th ed. Exeter:
                Ranlet and Norris, 1806. [S11769]
156. VH8   The Village Harmony, 8th ed. Exeter:
                Norris and Sawyer, 1807. [S14125]
157. VH9   The Village Harmony, 9th ed. Exeter:
                Norris and Sawyer, 1808. [S16636]
158. VH10   The Village Harmony, 10th ed. Exeter:
                Norris & Co., 1810. [S19115]
159. VH11   The Village Harmony, 11th ed.
                Newburyport: E. Little & Co., 1812.
                [27404]
160. VH12   The Village Harmony, 12th ed.
                Newburyport: E. Little & Co., 1815.
                [S36444]
161. VH13   The Village Harmony, 13th ed.
                Newburyport: E. Little & Co., 1816.
                [S39669]
162. VH14   The Village Harmony, 14th ed. Boston:
                West & Richardson, 1817 [S42790]
163. VH15   The Village Harmony, 15th ed. Exeter:
                J.J. Williams, 1818 [S46650]
164. VH16   The Village Harmony, 16th ed. Exeter:
                J.J. Williams, 1819 [S49993]
165. VH17   The Village Harmony, 17th ed. Exeter:
                J.J. Williams, 1820
166. WC1   The Worcester Collection of Sacred
                Harmony. Worcester: Isaiah Thomas,
                1786. [E19752]
167. WC2   The Worcester Collection of Sacred
                Harmony, 2d ed. Worcester: Isaiah
                Thomas, 1788. [E21193]
168. WC3   The Worcester Collection of Sacred
                Harmony, 3d ed. Boston: Thomas and
                Andrews, 1791. [E23490]
169. WC4   The Worcester Collection of Sacred
                Harmony, 4th ed. Boston: Thomas and
                Andrews, 1792. [E24461]
170. WC5   The Worcester Collection of Sacred
                Harmony, 5th ed. Boston: Thomas and
                Andrews, 1794. [E27202]

171. WC6   The Worcester Collection of Sacred
                  Harmony, 6th ed., ed. by Oliver Holden.
                  Boston: Thomas and Andrews, 1797.
                  [E32363]
172. WC7   The Worcester Collection of Sacred
                  Harmony, 7th ed., ed. by Oliver Holden.
                  Boston: Thomas and Andrews, 1800.
                  [E37786]
173. WC8   The Worcester Collection of Sacred
                  Harmony, 8th ed., ed. by Oliver Holden.
                  Boston: Thomas and Andrews, 1803.
                  [S4392]
174. WashburnPH   Washburn, Japheth Coombs. The Parish
                  Harmony. Exeter: C. Norris, 1813.
                  [S30447]
175. WestMC   West, Elisha. The Musical Concert.
                  Northampton: Andrew Wright, 1802.
                  [S3532]
176. WoodwardEH   Woodward, Charles. Ecclesiae Harmonia.
                  Philadelphia: [n.p.], 1807. [S14237]
177. WoodwardEH2 Woodward, Charles. Ecclesiae Harmonia,
                  2d ed. Philadelphia: [n.p.], 1809.
                  [S119262]
178. WyethRSM   Wyeth's Repository of Sacred Music.
                  Harrisburg: John Wyeth, 1810. [S22116]
179. WyethRSM5   Wyeth's Repository of Sacred Music, 5th
                  ed. Harrisburg: John Wyeth, 1820.
                  [S46885]
180. WyethRSM Pt2 Wyeth's Repository of Sacred Music, Part
                  Second. Harrisburg: John Wyeth, 1813.
                  [S30589]

                  II. British Tunebooks

ArnoldCP   Arnold, John. The Compleat Psalmodist,
                  4th ed. London: Robert Brown, 1756
KnappNCM   Knapp, William. New Church Melody, 2d
                  ed. London: R. Baldwin, 1754.

Lyra Davidica   <u>Lyra</u> <u>Davidica,</u> <u>or</u> <u>a</u> <u>Collection</u> <u>of</u> <u>Divine</u>
                       <u>Songs</u> <u>and</u> <u>Hymns</u>. London: J. Walsh,
                       1708.
Rippon Col   Rippon, John. <u>A</u> <u>Selection</u> <u>of</u> <u>Psalm</u> <u>and</u>
                       <u>Hymn</u> <u>Tunes</u>. London: the Author
                       [ca.1791]
Tans'urRMC   Tans'ur, William. <u>The</u> <u>Royal</u> <u>Melody</u>
                       <u>Compleat</u>. London: R. Brown, for James
                       Hodges, 1755.
WarnerSMG   Warner, Daniel. <u>Singing</u> <u>Masters</u> <u>Guide</u>.
                       London, 1719.
WilkinsBP   Wilkins, Matthew. <u>Book</u> <u>of</u> <u>Psalmody</u>.
                       Great Milton [n.p., ca. 1750]
WilliamsPE   Williams, T. <u>Psalmodia</u> <u>Evangelica</u>, 2
                       vols. London: S. A. and P. Thompson,
                       1789.

           III.   Collections of Hymns and Poems

Addison, Psalm   Addison, Joseph. A series of six psalm
                       and hymn versifications published in
                       1712 in <u>The</u> <u>Spectator</u>.
Bedford, <u>Specimen</u>   Bedford, Arthur. <u>The</u> <u>Excellency</u> <u>of</u>
                       <u>Divine</u> <u>Musick</u>. London: W. Pearson
                       [1733]. Appendix entitled: "A Specimen
                       of Hymns for Divine Musick."
Byles, <u>Pious</u>   [Byles, Samuel]. <u>Pious</u> <u>Remains</u> <u>of</u> <u>a</u>
                       <u>Young</u> <u>Gentleman</u> <u>Lately</u> <u>Remains</u>
                       <u>Deceased</u>. Boston: Richard Draper, 1764.
Byles, <u>Poems</u>   Byles, Mather. <u>Poems</u> <u>on</u> <u>Several</u>
                       <u>Occasions</u>. Boston: Kneeland and Green,
                       1744.
Brady and Tate   Brady, Nicholas, and Nahum Tate. <u>A</u> <u>New</u>
                       <u>Version</u> <u>of</u> <u>the</u> <u>Psalms</u> <u>of</u> <u>David</u>. London:
                       J. Roberts, 1749 (first published in
                       London, 1696). Some editions include "A
                       Supplement to the New Version of Psalms"
                       containing hymns.

Flatman, Poems   Flatman, Thomas. Poems and Songs.
                        London: for Benjamin Took, 1702.
Law, Collection   Law, Andrew. A Collection of Hymns for
                        Social Worship. [Connecticut, 1783].
Lyra Davidica   Lyra Davidica. London: J. Walsh,
                        1708.
Newton, Olney   Newton, John, and William Cowper. The
    Hymns   Olney Hymns. London: W. Oliver, 1779.
Peck, Description   Peck, John. A Description of the Last
                        Judgment, 2d ed. Philadelphia: Bell,
                        1773. (Includes "A Poem on Death" and
                        "On the Resurrection".)
Relly, Christian   Relly, James, and John Relly.
    Hymns   Christian Hymns, Poems, and Spiritual
                        Songs. London: M. Lewis, 1758.
Sternhold &   Sternhold, Thomas, John Hopkins, and
    Hopkins   others. The Booke of Psalms with
                        Hymnes Evangelical and Spiritual Songs.
                        London: Company of Stationers, 1621.
Watts, Divine   Watts, Isaac. Divine Songs Attempted
    Songs   in Easy Language for the Use of
                        Children, 16th ed. Philadelphia: Joseph
                        Crukshank for R. Aitken [1773].
Watts, Horae   Watts, Isaac. Horae Lyricae: Poems
    Lyricae   Chiefly of the Lyric Kind, 10th ed. New
                        York: Hugh Gaine, 1762 (first published
                        in London, 1706.
Watts, Hymns   Watts, Isaac. Hymns and Spiritual Songs
                        in Three Books. London: J. C. and F.
                        Rivington, 1788 (first published in
                        London, 1707-1709). Hymns I, Hymns II,
                        and Hymns III refer respectively to
                        Books I, II, and III.
Watts, Psalm   Watts, Isaac. The Psalms of David
                        Imitated in the Language of the New
                        Testament. London: J. C. and F.
                        Rivington, 1788. (first published in
                        London, 1719.
Wesley, Hymns   Wesley, Charles. Hymns and Sacred
                        Poems. Bristol: Felix Farley, 1749.

Whitefield,   Whitefield, George. A Collection
    Collection   of Hymns for Social Worship. London:
                       William Strahan, 1753.
Young, Complaint   Young, Edward. The Complaint, or Night
                       Thoughts. Philadelphia: Bell, 1777
                       (first published London, 1742-1745).

                    IV. Books and Articles

AndersonE   Anderson, Gillian B. "Eighteenth-
                       Century Evaluations of William Billings:
                       a Reappraisal," Quarterly Journal of
                       the Library of Congress, XXXV, no.1
                       (January 1978), pp.48-58.
AndersonFSC   Anderson, Gillian B. "The Funeral of
                       Samuel Cooper," The New England
                       Quarterly, v.50, no.4 (December 1977),
                       pp.644-659.
Atkins   Atkins, Charles L. "William Billings:
                       his Psalm and Hymn Tunes," in Addresses
                       at the International Hymnological
                       Conference, New York City, September 10-
                       11, 1961. New York: Hymn Society of
                       America, 1962, pp.3-16.
BarbourBB   Barbour, J. Murray. "Billings and the
                       Barline," American Choral Review, V,
                       no.2 (January 1963), pp.1-5.
BarbourCM   Barbour, J. Murray. The Church Music of
                       William Billings. East Lansing:
                       Michigan State University Press, 1960.
Boroff   Boroff, Edith. Music in Europe and the
                       United States. Englewood Cliffs, NJ:
                       Prentice-Hall, 1971.
Chase   Chase, Gilbert. America's Music, from
                       the Pilgrims to the Present, 3d ed.
                       Urbana: University of Illinois Press,
                       1987.
CrawfordCR   Crawford, Richard. The Core Repertory
                       of Early American Psalmody. Madison,

WI: A-R Editions, 1984. (Recent Researches in American Music, v.11-12.)

CrawfordMAB   Crawford, Richard. "Musicology and the Australian Bicentenary: a Methodological Prospectus from an American Viewpoint," Musicology Australia, VIII (1985), pp.2-13.

CrawfordMM   Crawford, Richard. "Massachusetts Musicians and the Core Repertory of Early American Psalmody," in Music and Musicians in Colonial Massachusetts, 2 vols. Boston: The Colonial Society of Massachusetts, 1985, II, 583-629.

Daniel   Daniel, Ralph T. The Anthem in New England Before 1800. Evanston: Northwestern University Press, 1966.

De Jong   De Jong, Mary Gosselink. "Both Pleasure and Profit": William Billings and the Uses of Music," William and Mary Quarterly, v.42, no.1 (January 1985), pp.104-116.

Gryc   Gryc, Stephen M. "Explicating William Billings's 'Jargon,'" In Theory Only, v.3, no.1 (April 1977), 22-28.

Hamm   Hamm, Charles. Music in the New World. New York: Norton, 1983.

HitchcockMUS   Hitchcock, H. Wiley. Music in the United States: a Historical Introduction. Englewood Cliffs, NJ: Prentice-Hall, 1969.

HitchcockWB   Hitchcock, H. Wiley. "William Billings and the Yankee Tunesmiths," Hi Fi/Stereo Review, XVI, no.2 (February 1966), pp.55-65.

Kingman   Kingman, Daniel. American Music: A Panorama. New York: Schirmer Books, 1979.

KroegerSIWP   Kroeger, Karl. "Settings of Isaac Watts's Psalm 50 by American Psalmodists," The Hymn, XLI, no.1 (January 1990), pp.19-27.

KroegerST   Kroeger, Karl. "Slur and Tie in Anglo-
                   American Psalmody," American Choral
                   Review, XXVIII, no.2 (April 1986),
                   pp.17-29.

KroegerWBHT   Kroeger, Karl. "William Billings and
                   the Hymn-Tune," The Hymn, XXXVII, no.3
                   (July 1986), pp.19-25.

KroegerWBM   Kroeger, Karl. "William Billings's
                   Music in Manuscript Copy and Some Notes
                   on Variant Versions of his Pieces,"
                   Notes, XXXIX, no.2 (December 1982),
                   pp.316-345.

KroegerWP   Kroeger, Karl. "Word Painting in the
                   Music of William Billings," American
                   Music, VI, no.1 (Spring 1988), pp.41-64.

Lawrence   Lawrence, Vera Brodsky. Music for
                   Patriots, Politicians, and Presidents.
                   New York: Macmillan, 1975.

Lindstrom   Lindstrom, Carl E. "William Billings
                   and his Times," The Musical Quarterly,
                   XXV, no.4 (October 1939), pp.479-497.

MacDougall   MacDougall, Hamilton C. Early New
                   England Psalmody. Brattleboro, VT:
                   Stephen Daye Press, 1940.

McKay   McKay, David P., and Richard Crawford.
                   William Billings of Boston. Princeton:
                   Princeton University Press, 1975.

Marrocco   Marrocco, W. Thomas, and Harold Gleason.
                   Music in America: an Anthology from the
                   Landing of the Pilgrims to the Close of
                   the Civil War, 1620-1865. New York:
                   W.W. Norton, 1964.

Mellers   Mellers, Wilfrid. Music in a New Found
                   Land: Themes and Developments in the
                   History of American Music. New York:
                   Hillstone, 1975.

NathanWB   Nathan, Hans. William Billings: Data
                   and Documents. Detroit: Information
                   Coordinators, 1976.

Schrader   Schrader, Arthur. "'Wilks,' 'No.45,'
                    and Mr. Billings," American Music, VII,
                    no.4 (Winter 1989), 412-429.
Stevenson   Stevenson, Robert. Protestant Church
                    Music in America. New York: W.W.
                    Norton, 1966.
WienandtAEA   Wienandt, Elwyn, and Robert H. Young.
                    The Anthem in England and America. New
                    York: Free Press, 1970.
WienandtBC   Wienandt, Elwyn. The Bicentennial
                    Collection of American Music. Carol
                    Stream, IL: Hope Publishing Co., 1974.

                    V. Manuscripts

Couch, North-   A separate manuscript compiled by W.
    western   Couch, Northwestern Harmony, 2 vols.,
    Harmony   at the John Hay Library, Brown
                    University, Providence, RI
Cowling   A separate manuscript entitled The
                    American Harmony compiled by Aaron
                    Cowling (ca.1798) at the American
                    Antiquarian Society, Worcester,
                    Massachusetts
CtHT-W Ms   A manuscript supplement to Thomas
                    Walter. The Grounds and Rules of Musick
                    Explained. Boston: for Samuel Gerrish,
                    1746, at the Watkinson Library, Trinity
                    College Hartford, Connecticut.
CtY Ms   A manuscript supplement to William
                    Tans'ur, The American Harmony,
                    Newburyport: Daniel Bayley, 1771, at the
                    Yale University Library, New Haven,
                    Connecticut.
DLC Ms   A manuscript supplement to William
                    Tans'ur, The Royal Melody Complete, 3d
                    ed. Boston: William M'Alpine, 1767, at
                    the Library of Congress, Washington, DC.

MHi Ms   A separate manuscript entitled "Ms
                        Music by Shepard Fish. 1730" at the
                        Massachusetts Historical Society,
                        Boston.

MiU-C Ms1   A manuscript supplement to William
                        Billings. The New-England
                        Psalm-Singer. Boston: Edes and Gill,
                        [1770] at the William L. Clements
                        Library, The University of Michigan, Ann
                        Arbor.

MiU-C Ms2   A manuscript supplement to William
                        Billings. The Singing Master's
                        Assistant. Boston: Draper and Folsom,
                        1778, at the William L. Clements
                        Library, The University of Michigan, Ann
                        Arbor.

MiU-C Ms3   Musical additions to a manuscript
                        orderly book written by Eleazer
                        Everett at Francistown, New Hampshire,
                        at the William L. Clements Library, The
                        University of Michigan, Ann Arbor.

MSaE Ms1   A manuscript supplement to William
                        Tans'ur. The American Harmony.
                        Newburyport: Daniel Bayley, 1769, at the
                        Essex Institute, Salem, Massachusetts.

MSaE Ms2   A manuscript supplement to William
                        Tans'ur. The American Harmony.
                        Newburyport: Daniel Bayley, 1771, at the
                        Essex Institute, Salem, Massachusetts.

MWA Ms   A manuscript supplement to William
                        Tans'ur. The Royal Melody Compleat, 4th
                        ed. Newburyport: Daniel Bayley, 1768,
                        at the American Antiquarian Society,
                        Worcester, Massachusetts.

NN Ms1   A manuscript supplement to William
                        Tans'ur. The American Harmony.
                        [Newburyport: Daniel Bayley, 1773] at
                        the Americana Collection, Music
                        Division, New York Public Library.

NN Ms2   A manuscript supplement to William
                        Billings. The New-England

	Psalm-Singer. Boston: Edes and Gill, [1770], at the Americana Collection, Music Division, New York Public Library.
RPB Ms	A manuscript supplement to Daniel Bayley. _A New and Complete Introduction to the Grounds and Rules of Musick._ Boston: Thomas Johnston, 1766, at the Harris Collection, John Hay Library, Brown University, Providence, Rhode Island.
Rutgers Ms	A manuscript supplement to Daniel Read. _The Columbian Harmonist No.1_. New Haven: the Author, [1793] at the Rutgers University Library, New Brunswick, New Jersey.
Waterhouse Ms	A separate music manuscript entitled "Sukey Heath's 1st July 1782 Collection from Sundry Authors" in the possession of Mrs. Dorothy Waterhouse, Boston, Massachusetts.

VI. Recordings

A. _Pleasure Tunes My Tongue: Folk Hymns and Anthems from the Sacred Harp Tradition_. One Accord; Kathleen Thro, dir. Alexianna Records AR 1001 (1988)

B. _A Christmas Potpourri_. Colonial Williamsburg WS115 (1984)

C. _Christmas in the New World_. Musical Heritage Society MHS4077 (1979)

D. _Harp of Joy_. Chancel Choir of Plymouth Church, Shaker Heights, Ohio; John D. Herr, dir. Musical Heritage Society MHS4070 (1979)

E. _Make a Joyful Noise: Mainstreams and Backwaters of American Psalmody_. New World Records NWR255 (1978)

F. _A Garden Concert of American Choral Music in Memory of Ericsson Foote Bushnell_. Golden Crest CRS4172 (1977)

G. _White Spirituals From the Sacred Harp_. New World Records   NWR205 (1977)

H. America Sings. Vol.I: The Founding Years. Gregg Smith
    Singers; Gregg Smith, dir.   Vox Productions SVBX5350-2
    (1976)

I. The Birth of Liberty: Music of the American
    Revolution. New World Records NWR276 (1976)

J. Be Glad Then America. London Records OS26442 (1975)

K. Sing We At Pleasure. Advent Records 5018 (1975)

L. Early American Vocal Music: New England Anthems and
    Southern Folk Hymns. The Western Wind Vocal Ensemble.
    Nonesuch Records H-71276 (1973)

M. American Music Group, Vol.4 LPS 260 04 (1972)

N. American Colonial Christmas Music. Musical Heritage
    Society MHS1126 (1970)

O. Fasola: 53 Shaped-Note Folk Hymns. Asch Records
    AHM4151 (1970)

P. Choral Rarities. Desto Records DC102 (197?)

Q. O Come, Sweet Music: Part Songs of the Colonial
    Period. Colonial Williamsburg 102 (197?)

R. The Continental Harmony: The Music of William
    Billings. The Gregg Smith Singers; Gregg Smith, cond.
    Columbia Records MS7277 (1969)

S. New England Harmony. The Old Sturbridge Singers; Floyd
    Corson, dir. Folkways Records FA2377 (1964)

T. Music in America: Choral Music in Colonial America.
    Society for the Preservation of the American Musical
    Heritage MIA114 (1963)

U. The Sounds of History. Time, Inc. LHS002 (1963)

V. A Choral Concert. Desto Records D102 (1962?)

W. What Wondrous Love. The Robert Shaw Chorale; Robert
    Shaw, dir. RCA Victor Records LM2403 (1960)

X. Christmas Carols in Cambridge. Cambridge Records
    CRS104 (196?)

Y. Heritage: American ballads and songs, 1750-1840.
    Robert De Cormier Folk Singers. Command Records
    RS884SD (196?)

Z. The Lord's Prayer. The Mormon Tabernacle Choir.
    Columbia Records ML5386 (1959)

AA. Sacred Harp Singing. Library of Congress Records AAFS
    L11 (1959)

AB. Presenting the Belafonte Singers. RCA Victor Records
    LPM1760 (1958)

AC. A Treasury of Easter Songs. RCA Victor Records LM1201
     (1958)
AD. Christmas Hymns and Carols, Vol.1. The Robert Shaw
     Chorale; Robert Shaw, dir. RCA Victor Records LM2139
     (1957)
AE. Robert Shaw Conducts Christmas Hymns and Carols,
     Vol.2. The Robert Shaw Chorale; Robert Shaw, cir. RCA
     Victor Records LM1711 (1952)
AF. American Songs. The Robert Shaw Chorale; Robert Shaw,
     dir. RCA Victor Records LM57 (1951)
AG. Promised Land. Lyrichord Records LL64 (195?)
AH. American Song Album. Columbia Records MM329 (194?)
AI. American Music. American Heritage Records P2-11687
     (n.d.)
AJ. A Christmas Sing-In. RCA Victrola Records VIC1509
     (n.d.)
AK. English Madrigals and American Part Songs. Concert
     Hall Records CHC52 (n.d.)
AL. Golden Ring: A Gathering of Friends for Making Music.
     Folk-Legacy Records FSI-16 (n.d.)
AM. This is My Country. The Robert Shaw Chorale; Robert
     Shaw, dir. RCA Victor Records LM2662 (n.d.)
AN. The American Harmony. Chapel Choir, University of
     Maryland; Fague Springman, dir. Washington Records WR-
     418 (n.d.)
AO. The Madrigalists. Columbia Records M434 (n.d.)
AP. The Songs of Early America. Elie Siegmeister Singers;
     Elie Siegmeister, dir. Bost Records ES1 (n.d.)
AQ. The Madrigal Singers. Lehman Engel, dir. Columbia
     Records M329 (n.d.)
AR. All Day Singing from "The Sacred Harp". Alabama Sacred
     Harp Singers. Prestige International Records 25007
     (n.d.)
AS. An Appeal to Heaven. Old Stoughton Musical Society.
     Old Northbridge Records ONB1762 (1975)
AT. Songs of Liberty: Music of the Revolutionary War.
     Choir of the Bruton Parish Church; J. S. Darling, dir.
     Colonial Williamsburg Records WS106 (1975)
AU. Music of the American Revolution. The Colonial Singers
     and Players; Gillian Anderson, dir. Colonial Singers
     and Players Record [no number] (1975)

First Line Index

Anthem Title Index

A Funeral Anthem Rev. Chap. 14th.	I Heard A Great Voice
A FUNERAL ANTHEM. Words from Sundry scriptures.	Samuel The Priest
An Anthem	Thou, O God, Art Praised
An Anthem Isaiah 55	Let Ev'ry Mortal Ear Attend
An Anthem. Joel 1st and 2d Chap. Suitable for Fast.	Sanctify A Fast
An Anthem. Psalm 18	The Lord Descended From Above
An Anthem Psalm 39th.	Hear My Prayer, O Lord
An Anthem Psalm 42	As The Hart Panteth
An Anthem. Psalm 44th.	We Have Heard With Our Ears
An Anthem. Psalm 47. For Thanksgiving.	O Clap Your Hands
An Anthem. Psalm 81st.	Sing Ye Merrily
An Anthem. Psalm 93	The Lord Is King
An Anthem. Psalm 103	Praise The Lord, O My Soul
An Anthem. Psalm 108. For Thanksgiving Day Morning.	O God, My Heart Is Fixed
An Anthem. Psalm 126	When The Lord Turn'd Again
An Anthem Psalm 127	Except The Lord Build The House
An Anthem Psalm the 143 for Fast Day	Hear My Prayer, O Lord
An Anthem. Revns Chap 5th	And I Saw A Mighty Angel
An Anthem. 2d Samuel Chap. 1st.	The Beauty of Israel

An Anthem. Solomon's Songs	I Charge You, O Ye Daughters
An Anthem Solomon's Songs, Chap. 2	I Am The Rose Of Sharon
An Anthem Solomons' Songs, Chap. 5th	I Am Come Into My Garden
An Anthem. Words by Dr. Watts.	Lift Up Your Eyes
An Anthem For Christmas	Hark! Hark! Hear You Not
An Anthem for Easter.	The Lord Is Ris'n Indeed
An Anthem For Fast Day	Hear, Hear, O Heav'ns
An Anthem for Fast Day.	Mourn, Mourn
An Anthem for Ordination.	O Thou To Whom All Creatures Bow
An Anthem for Thanksgiving. Psalm 148.	O Praise The Lord Of Heaven
An Anthem. For Thanksgiving Day Morning.	Sing Praises To The Lord
Anthem taken from Mathew 5 & 25 1 Chorin Chap 13 & 14 Psalm 34 & 41.	Blessed Is He That Considereth the Poor
An Anthem Taken From Sundry Scriptures	Is Any Afflicted; Who Is This That Cometh From Edom
An Anthem taken from Sundry scriptures for Charity meetings.	Blessed Is He That Considereth the Poor
CONSONANCE An Anthem.	Down Steers The Bass
DAVID'S LAMENTATION	David, The King, Was Grieved
DELIVERANCE, An Anthem.	I Will Love Thee
EUROCLYDON, An Anthem. Psalm 107 for Mariners.	They That Go Down To The Sea
GRATITUDE. An Anthem. Psalm 116th	I Love The Lord
INDEPENDENCE	The States, O Lord
LAMENTATION OVER BOSTON.	By The Rivers of Watertown
MODERN MUSICK	We Are Met For A Concert
PEACE, An Anthem.	God Is The King
RETROSPECT, An Anthem from Sundry Scriptures	Was Not The Day Dark And Gloomy
SUBLIMITY. An Anthem. Psalm 19.	The Heavens Declare
THE DYING CHRISTIAN TO HIS SOUL.	Vital Spark Of Heav'nly Flame
THE DYING CHRISTIAN'S LAST FAREWELL	My Friends, I Am Going
UNION. An Anthem. Psalm 133.	Behold How Good And Joyful

Text Source Index

Billings, William?	CONNECTION, EMANUEL, EUROPE, HANOVER, INVOCATION, LIBERTY, WILLIAMSBURGH; Mourn, Mourn; O Praise God; Was Not The Day Dark And Gloomy; We Are Met For A Concert
Book of Common Prayer	Behold How Good And Joyful; Except The Lord Build The House; God Is The King; O God, My Heart Is Fixed, O God, Thou Hast Been Displeased; O Praise God; O Praise The Lord Of Heaven; O Thou To Whom All Creatures Bow; Praise The Lord, O My Soul; Sing Praises To The Lord; Sing Ye Merrily; The Heavens Declare; They That Go Down To The Sea; Thou, O God, Art Praised; When The Lord Turn'd Again
Brady & Tate Psalms	AMHERST, ASHFORD, BENEFICENCE, BENEVOLENCE, THE BIRD, BROOKLINE, HAVERILL, LEWIS-TOWN, MALDEN, MANCHESTER, MARBLEHEAD, MARSHFIELD, MILTON, NEW BOSTON, NEW NORTH, NEW PLYMOUTH, NEW SOUTH, PHILADELPHIA, PLYMOUTH NEW, POMFRET, PRINCETOWN, PUMPILY, ROXBURY, ST. ENOCH, SMITHFIELD, STOCKBRIDGE, TAUNTON, UNION, WHEELER'S POINT, O Thou To Whom All Creatures Bow; The States, O Lord
Brady & Tate Supplement	BETHLEHEM, HYMN FOR CHRISTMAS, KITTERY
Byles, Mather	CANON 6 IN 1, HOLLIS STREET, THOMAS TOWN, Down Steers The Bass
Byles, Samuel	MEDFIELD
Earl of Roscommon	O Praise The Lord Of Heaven
Flatman, Thomas	HEATH, MORPHEUS
Ken, Thomas	Behold How Good And Joyful
Morton, Perez	CANON 4 IN 1, CORSICA, EMMAUS, MASSACHUSETTS, QUEEN STREET, WALTHAM, WILKS, O Clap Your Hands

Watts, Psalms	ADAMS, ASSURANCE, BRADFORD, BRATTLE STREET, CAMBRIDGE, CAMDEN, CHOCKSETT, COBHAM, CONNECTION, CREATION, DEDHAM, DUNSTABLE, DUXBOROUGH, EAST SUDBURY, EGYPT, HALIFAX, LEWIS-TOWN, MANSFIELD, MEDWAY, PHOEBUS, PSALM 18, RALEIGH, REVELATION, RUTLAND, SHEFFIELD, SHERBURNE, SPAIN, STOCKBRIDGE, UNION, VICTORY, WALTHAM, WASHINGTON, WRENTHAM, I Will Love Thee; The States, O Lord
Wesley, Charles	ST. PETER'S
Whitefield, Collection	BOLTON, HOLLIS STREET, HOPKINTON, ROCHESTER, SAVANNAH, WARREN
Young, Edward	The Lord Is Ris'n Indeed

Tune Type Index

Antiphonal Plain Tune	CHELSEA, MIDDLESEX, SAVANNAH
Fuging Chorus	ADORATION, ANDOVER, AURORA, BETHLEHEM, THE BIRD, BRATTLE STREET, COHASSET, CREATION, CRUCIFICTION, DARTMOUTH, DEDHAM, DUNSTABLE, EUROPE, FRAMINGHAM, GREAT PLAIN, INVOCATION, MANCHESTER, MARYLAND, MEDWAY, MILTON, NEW PLYMOUTH, PHILADELPHIA, ST. ANDREWS, TAUNTON, WAREHAM, WASHINGTON STREET, WEYMOUTH, WHEELER'S POINT
Fuging Tune, Antiphonal	HEBRON, HOPKINTON
Fuging Tune, Double	ASSURANCE, SHEFFIELD
Fuging Tune, Plain	BENEVOLENCE, BROAD COVE, EGYPT, GILEAD, HADLEY, HEATH, KITTERY, MORNING HYMN, NORTHBOROUGH, NORTH PROVIDENCE, REDEMPTION, ROCKY NOOK, ST. ENOCH, WASHINGTON
Plain tune	AFRICA, ALBANY, AMERICA, ANDOVER, ASHHAM, ASIA,

Plain tune (cont.)

ATTLEBOROUGH, BARRE, BEDFORD, BENNINGTON, BRAINTREE, BRATTLE SQUARE, BRATTLE STREET, BRIDGWATER, BROOKFIELD, BROOKLINE, CALVARY, CAMBRIDGE, CANON of 4 in 1, CANON of 6 in 1, CHELSEA, CHESTER, CHESTERFIELD, CONCORD, CONNECTION, CREATION, CRUCIFICTION, CUMBERLAND, DANBURY, DEDHAM, DELAWARE, DICKINSON, DIGHTON, DORCHESTER, DUBLIN, DUDLEY, DUNSTABLE, DUXBOROUGH, EASTHAM, EAST-TOWN, EDEN, ELECTION, EMMAUS, ESSEX, EUROPE, FAIRFIELD, FITCHBURGH, FRAMINGHAM, FRANKLIN, FREEDOM, FRIENDSHIP, GEORGIA, GLOCESTER, GREENLAND, HALIFAX, HAMPSHIRE, HAMTON, HANOVER, HANOVER NEW, HARVARD, HATFIELD, HEBRON, HINGHAM, HOLDEN, HOLLIS, HOLLIS STREET, IPSWICH, JAMAICA, JARGON, JERUSALEM, LANCASTER, LEBANON, LEXINGTON, LIBERTY, LINCOLN, LYNN, MADRID, MALDEN, MANCHESTER, MANSFIELD, MARBLEHEAD, MARSHFIELD, MASSACHUSETTS, MEDFIELD, MEDFORD, MIDDLETOWN, MORIAH, MORPHEUS, MORRISTON, NANTASKET, NANTUCKET, NAZARETH, NEW BOSTON, NEW CASTLE, NEW HAVEN, NEW HINGHAM, NEW NORTH, NEW SOUTH, NEW TOWN, NEWBURN, NEWPORT, NORTH RIVER, NUTFIELD, OLD BRICK, OLD SOUTH, ORANGE STREET, ORLEANS, OXFORD,

Plain tune (cont.)   PARIS, PEMBROKE, PEMBROKE NEW,
                            PLAINFIELD, PLEASANT STREET,
                            PLYMTON, POMFRET, POWNALL,
                            PRINCETOWN, PROVIDENCE, PSALM
                            18, PURCHASE STREET, RALEIGH,
                            REVELATION, ROXBURY, ST.
                            ELISHA'S, ST. JOHN'S, ST.
                            PETER'S, ST. VINCENT'S,
                            SAYBROOK, SCITUATE, SHERBURNE,
                            SHIRLEY, SPAIN, SPENCER,
                            STOUGHTON, STURBRIDGE,
                            SUDBURY, SUFFOLK, SULLIVAN,
                            SUMMER STREET, SWANZEY, TOWER
                            HILL, TRINITY NEW, UNION,
                            UNITY, UXBRIDGE, WALTHAM,
                            WAREHAM, WATER TOWN,
                            WELLFLEET, WESTFIELD,
                            WHEELLER'S POINT, WILKS,
                            WILLIAMSBURGH, WRENTHAM
Set Piece   BERLIN, RUTLAND
Tune with Extension   ADAMS, AMHERST, BALTIMORE,
                            BOSTON, BRATTLE STREET,
                            BRUNSWICK, CHOCKSETT,
                            CLAREMONT, COLUMBIA, CONQUEST,
                            CONSOLATION, CORSICA, EAST
                            SUDBURY, EXETER, GOLGOTHA,
                            GOSPEL POOL, HATFIELD, HULL,
                            HYMN FOR CHRISTMAS, MANSFIELD,
                            MENDOM, MORAVIA, NORFOLK, NO.
                            45, OLD NORTH, PETERSBURGH,
                            PHOEBUS, PITT, PUMPILY, QUEEN
                            STREET, RESIGNATION,
                            RESTORATION, RESURRECTION, ST.
                            THOMAS, SAPPHO, SHARON, SOUTH
                            BOSTON, SUNDAY, THOMAS TOWN,
                            VERMONT, WARREN, WEST SUDBURY,
                            WORCESTER
Tune with Extension,   BELLINGHAM, BOLTON,
    Antiphonal   BURLINGTON, COBHAM, HARTFORD,
                            HEBRON, JORDAN, THE LARK,

Tune with Extension, Antiphonal (Cont.)	LEWIS-TOWN, MAJESTY, PHYLANTHROPY, PLYMOUTH NEW, ROCHESTER, SUDBURY, UNION, VICTORY
Verse & Chorus, Antiphonal	ASHFORD, BENEFICENCE, CAMDEN, CROSS STREET, GERMANTOWN, HACKER'S HALL, HAVERILL, JUDEA, SHILOH, SMITHFIELD, STOCKBRIDGE
Verse & Chorus, Extended	BAPTISM, BRADFORD, EMANUEL, RICHMOND, SINAI, WEST BOSTON,

Incipit Index

About the Compiler

KARL KROEGER is Professor and Music Librarian at the University of Colorado, Boulder. He was editor of three volumes of *The Complete Works of William Billings,* and his articles have appeared in *Bach, American Music,* and *Notes.* He has also made contributions to the *New Grove Dictionary of Music and Musicians* and the *New Grove Dictionary of American Music.*